"The last few years have witnessed a flu
tian view of work. This is the best of t
comprehensive, theologically informec.
now the 'must-read' volume on the subject."
> —**D. A. Carson**, Emeritus Professor of New Testament, Trinity
> Evangelical Divinity School

"For everyone everywhere, our work is an expression of how we answer the most complex questions of life, of who we are and why we are. A historian, a theologian, an ethicist, a pastor, and (perhaps most profoundly) a grandfather, Dan Doriani takes up this complexity with seasoned wisdom born of years of paying attention to the life he has lived and the labor he has done. This volume is a unique contribution to the growing literature on the meaning of work for human beings. At one and the same time it is rooted in remarkably rich biblical and theological reflection and also pastorally responsive to the people Dan has known whose vocational questions have informed his writing. I know of no other book like *Work*. May it have a wide reading among those who wrestle with why we work, and why our work matters to God and the world."
> —**Steven Garber**, Professor of Marketplace Theology, Regent College; author, *Visions of Vocation: Common Grace for the Common Good*

"Only recently has the evangelical church begun to pay attention to the challenge of discipling Christians for their public life and, in particular, to the integration of their faith with their vocations and work lives. Dan Doriani's book makes an important contribution to this literature. Dan is an academic who wears his considerable scholarship lightly as he writes a theologically rich but accessible book on the Christian and work. His clear teaching on how faithful work leads to social reform is especially provocative and helpful."
> —**Timothy Keller**, Founding Pastor, Redeemer Presbyterian Church, Manhattan; Chairman and Cofounder, Redeemer City to City (CTC)

"I am grateful for mentors such as Dan Doriani, whose insights draw us back to the truths that guide us in loving God and living well. In this latest volume, Dan reminds us that the *first* 'Great Commission' happened in Genesis, when God charged Adam and Eve (and us) to tend God's garden and exercise dominion over his creation. With characteristic wisdom and practical guidance, Dan paints a compelling vision for all good work. He also dismantles the false dichotomy between work that is 'sacred' and work that is 'secular'—for God has instilled creative and redemptive significance in the calling of executives, artists, sanitation workers, landscapers, and homemakers, just as he has done for pastors and missionaries. Together, we are all commissioned and 'sent' workers in God's field. For these and many other reasons, I highly commend this book."

—**Scott Sauls**, Senior Pastor, Christ Presbyterian Church, Nashville, Tennessee; author, *From Weakness to Strength* and *Irresistible Faith*

"I love my friend's new book! Dan was teaching on the relationship between faith, work, and culture long before this topic became popular. So as I read these chapters, it was like savoring a vintage wine—the fruit of time, reflection, and distillation. With a high view of creation, a great love for the gospel, and the hope of Christ's kingdom stirring in his heart, Dan has given us a wonderful introduction to a biblical theology of work. It is accessible, practical, and brimming with Dan's wonderful personality."

—**Scotty Smith**, Pastor Emeritus, Christ Community Church, Franklin, Tennessee; Teacher in Residence, West End Community Church, Nashville, Tennessee

"A concise yet comprehensive must-read for the thoughtful and committed Christian embedded in the 'secular' workplace. Dan Doriani has masterfully captured the nuances of the twenty-first-century workaday world, covering a wide range of topics from discerning God's calling to dealing with difficult corporate situations and contemporary dilemmas, such as overwork and underemployment. Doriani skillfully explains pertinent theological principles in everyday language, lacing his narrative with compelling true-life illustrations and applications. Whether answering God's calling on the shop floor, in the corporate office, or in the home, the reader will find practical and theologically sound answers here."

—**Franz J. Wippold II**, Emeritus Professor of Radiology, Washington University, St. Louis

WORK

WORK

ITS PURPOSE,
DIGNITY, AND
TRANSFORMATION

DANIEL M. DORIANI

PUBLISHING
P.O. BOX 817 • PHILLIPSBURG • NEW JERSEY 08865-0817

Printed in the United States of America

ISBN: 978-1-62995-559-9 (pbk)
ISBN: 978-1-62995-628-2 (ePub)
ISBN: 978-1-62995-629-9 (Mobi)

Library of Congress Cataloging-in-Publication Data

Names: Doriani, Daniel M., 1953- author.
Title: Work : its purpose, dignity, and transformation / Daniel M. Doriani.
Description: Phillipsburg : P&R Publishing, 2019. | Includes bibliographical
references and index.
Identifiers: LCCN 2018042749| ISBN 9781629955599 (pbk.) | ISBN 9781629956282
(epub) | ISBN 9781629956299 (mobi)
Subjects: LCSH: Work--Religious aspects--Christianity.
Classification: LCC BT738.5 .D67 2019 | DDC 261.8/5--dc23
LC record available at https://lccn.loc.gov/2018042749

For Estelle and Jonah
May you always love reading in the company of friends.
To you I dedicate this book.

CONTENTS

FOREWORD

In his excellent *Work: Its Purpose, Dignity, and Transformation*, my friend Dan Doriani states that he has written this for "all who want to practice love and justice in their work, whether they be professionals or laborers, business leaders or artisans, students, retirees, or stay-at-home parents." He especially focuses on two kinds of people:

> The first kind doubts the value of their labor. When asked about their work, they often begin with two words: "I just." They say, "I just watch children," "I just stock shelves," "I just market clothing," or "I just transport vegetables." Yes, but anyone who ships vegetables efficiently makes life better for numerous people, many of them poor. That said, I'm no "Your work matters" cheerleader. Indeed, some work is so shoddy and trivial that it barely seems to matter.

The second kind of person is typified by

> the woman who ardently yearns to do significant work, the man who dares to think his work can change his corner of the world. In this, I join John Calvin, Abraham Kuyper, and their followers as they affirm that Jesus is Lord of every domain, not merely the church. Jesus declares that he rules everything when he says that the kingdom of God has *arrived* (Matt. 12:28; Luke 11:20). When the Gospels *show* Jesus working, whether

teaching crowds or healing the sick, the physicality of his activity demonstrates that redemption reshapes all of life—the body, not just the spirit.

Work will equip menial laborers and potential world-transformers to glorify God in all they do; to see how their Christian faith should shape their work globally, no matter what their jobs; and to understand how Christ's kingdom can be manifested in *all* their labors and undertakings.

When you begin to recognize the aspects of your vocation that can honor God, then you see that that all kinds of work possess qualities of dignity—not just the jobs of preachers or presidents, and not just those of CEOs and surgeons. God is calling the cop and the carpenter and the concrete layer to experience the dignity of their work as he uses their jobs to help others, improve lives, and spread the influence of his kingdom in the world—in the skills they express, in the products they make, in the way they work, in the impact of their labors on society, and in the relationships affected by their work.

An early description of how society began to flourish and diversify with God's blessing is found in Genesis 4:19–22: "Lamech took two wives. The name of the one was Adah, and the name of the other Zillah. Adah bore Jabal; he was the father of those who dwell in tents and have livestock. His brother's name was Jubal; he was the father of all those who play the lyre and pipe. Zillah also bore Tubal-cain; he was the forger of all instruments of bronze and iron."

In this description of the very earliest stages of human history, we find God's creativity and expanding blessings being expressed in the diverse professions and vocations of his people. Some are raising livestock. Others are musicians. Some are craftsmen or metalworkers. All these different professions are being established as the means by which society is advancing under God's plan—a plan honoring every vocation that furthers God's purposes.

Dan concludes *Work* by saying that despite human sin, the cultural mandate (that is, God's charge to the first humans to govern and develop the earth) still stands. Because Christ, the King, has come, his kingdom has arrived; his lordship is to be manifest in every realm of life, including our work. Work is not merely about making a living while avoiding sin; it about extending the kingdom rule of the Lord Jesus Christ.

I heartily recommend *Work* to all Christians who long to understand how their occupations and vocations fit into God's great kingdom plan.

Bryan Chapell
Pastor, Grace Presbyterian Church
President Emeritus, Covenant Theological Seminary

PREFACE

I earned my first legal paycheck in 1970, when I lived on the coast in North Carolina and worked at the improbably named but immensely popular Sanitary Restaurant. The restaurant sat on the water, so fishing boats could dock at the back in the late afternoon and early evening. At best, they moved fish and shrimp from the open sea to the dinner plate in less than an hour. The décor was simple, the prices were low, and the lines stretched around the block on weekends. I was a lowly kitchen hand, slopping plates and loading the dishwasher in a steamy, undersized space. During peak hours, our equipment couldn't manage the load. When the overburdened garbage disposal choked on discarded food, it made an ominous "wub-wub-wub" sound, and then belched, spraying fragments of fish, French fries, and hush puppies onto our aprons, faces, and hair. Some nights, we had to throw food into trash cans. When they filled, we tossed the refuse from every fourth or fifth plate on the floor. When the slop was ankle-deep, we threw wooden pallets over it in order to walk safely. Once, a pallet submerged into the accumulating muck, and we added a second. After the rush, we lifted and washed the pallets and shoveled smashed fish and fries into the now-docile disposal. The experience gave ample food for thought. Why did we *like* the explosions of fish debris? Why were those terrible nights so exhilarating? Why did we feel like conquerors afterward? Why didn't the restaurant raise its prices marginally and improve the kitchen?

Work has always fascinated me. As a child, I learned that one of my grandfathers had been a farmer and the other a musician. Both seemed marvelous. I enjoyed interviewing hundreds of people about their work, whether for this book or during my years as lead pastor at a large, professionally diverse church. Work demands deep training and absorbs vast energy. At work, we prove and improve ourselves, even find ourselves. If not, at least we earn a living.

In this book I hope to engage all who want to practice love and justice in their work, whether they be professionals or laborers, business leaders or artisans, students, retirees, or stay-at-home parents. Still, I especially write for two kinds of people. The first kind doubts the value of their labor. When asked about their work, they often begin with two words: "I just." They say, "I just watch children," "I just stock shelves," "I just market clothing," or "I just transport vegetables." Yes, but anyone who ships vegetables efficiently makes life better for numerous people, many of them poor. That said, I'm no "Your work matters" cheerleader. Indeed, some work is so shoddy and trivial that it barely seems to matter.

I also write for a second kind of person, the woman who ardently yearns to do significant work, the man who dares to think his work can change his corner of the world. In this, I join John Calvin, Abraham Kuyper, and their followers as they affirm that Jesus is Lord of every domain, not merely the church. Jesus declares that he rules everything when he says that the kingdom of God has *arrived* (Matt. 12:28; Luke 11:20). When the Gospels *show* Jesus working, whether teaching crowds or healing the sick, the physicality of his activity demonstrates that redemption reshapes all of life—the body, not just the spirit.

I write as a theologian, but for most of my career, I have taught New Testament and biblical interpretation and preached expository sermons from Scripture. This book is therefore grounded in the text of Scripture. I generally give the results, not the process of the exegetical work, but readers will detect signs of the process when I switch translations. I generally prefer the ESV translation, which is accurate and reliable. I quote others when they seem to best convey the sense of the Hebrew or Greek original. I sometimes quote two translations because each presents a vital dimension of the text. The goal is always to communicate the sense of Scripture, especially as it shapes our understanding of work.

I explain the twelve principles guiding this book at the end of chapter 1. One principle stands behind them all, the conviction that a biblical theology of work begins with the character of God. We are creative because God is creative. We long to fix what is broken because he planned to heal this aching world. We love to finish a task, even if it requires suffering, because Jesus finished the task of redemption, at great cost. So the character of God shapes the character of our work.

My interests reveal themselves in the plan for this monograph. Chapters 1–4 are foundational. They define work, summarize the biblical teaching on it, and explore the most influential theories of work. Chapters 5–8 address core topics: calling, faithfulness, work amid hardship, and the rhythm of work and rest. The last two chapters explore the way in which Christians strive to reform the workplace or society at large. Those chapters offer a theology or apologetic for the project of attempting to bring reformation through work. Finally, the appendix offers biblical principles for ten common fields of labor.

ACKNOWLEDGMENTS

Like every author, I have an army of friends and allies who deserve my gratitude. First, I thank Jack White, Robert Tweed, and Pete Steen of Geneva College for introducing me to the social implications of Calvinism, and I thank my classmates Tim and Tom Bennett, Mike Foyle, and Jim Dittmar for the first battles over "Christian lightbulbs." I am grateful to the leaders of Covenant Seminary for a job description that includes writing as a duty and grants me time to fulfill it. We don't have research professors, but this comes close. Many other friends removed flaws, improved the style, and added helpful thoughts to this book. Of them, Jay Wippold, Robbie Griggs, Vicki Tatko, John Hughes, and Debbie Doriani deserve singular praise.

If this book has a distinctive flavor, it is due to the dozens of people who sat for official interviews and the hundreds who endured strings of question in rambling, informal sessions. Special thanks to Abby, Debbie, Nancy 1 and Nancy 2, Sarah, Shelley, Bill, Bruce, Dave, David, Gerry, Joe 1 and Joe 2, Rand, Russ, and Tyler for sharing your insights again and again. Hundreds of students listened to parts of this book in lectures; their questions, objections, and suggestions made this work stronger, as did the feedback from everyone who worked through early drafts and pushed me to do better.

This book was delayed, but its scribe was happier, due to the sweet distractions afforded by Estelle and Jonah in their regular, if extralegal, visits to my home office. Jonah, thanks for bringing me book after book to read before your afternoon naps. And Estelle, thanks for the way you held my hands and shouted for joy the day you found out that I don't just read books—I write them.

My hope, when I start to read a book, is that I will learn something on every page. I learned more than I expected as I wrote this book, and I pray that you, O reader, will learn and, if possible, find courage to act through these pages.

PART 1

FOUNDATIONS

1

INTRODUCTION

The Personal Nature of Work

We spend most of our waking hours working. At work we fulfill many of our noblest dreams and endure many of our greatest sorrows. At work we do things *for* people and we do things *to* people, and they return the favor. Through work we feed our families and serve our neighbors. Through work we hone skills and make friends. When we work, we face our sin and the world's brokenness, and yet we discover grounds for hope. Mindless work crushes the soul; yet even in the midst of tedious work, we may find ourselves and our place in society. I did.

My story of work begins with my father. He had enough charm and intelligence to land any job he wanted, and he did so, whether in government, construction, higher education, or the church. However, his self-discipline did not match his gifts, so he found it easier to get a job than to keep one. His setbacks troubled him, and he took out his frustrations on me, perhaps because he saw traces of himself in me. Over and over he told me that I was lazy, worthless, good for nothing, and that I always would be. Perhaps he was projecting his fears about himself onto me, but as a child, I could not see that. Children assume that whatever their parents say must be true. Besides, the charge of laziness was fair at times.

In college I began to work as if bent on avenging every lost hour and silencing my father. My mentors taught me that God

3

intends to redeem all of life, and I dared to believe my labors could change the world. I resolved to become a professor and tore through graduate programs at great speed while neglecting things like sleep.

I've probably worked too hard ever since, toiling as professor, pastor, academic leader, speaker, writer, editor, and unlicensed and unpaid counselor. While in school, I washed dishes, sold hardware, tended machines, prepared food, harvested crops, unloaded trucks, guarded factories, and either painted or demolished buildings, as bosses decreed. I found particular delight in teaching—so much so, that I would do it for free if I never had to grade exams. My motives have been mixed, as motives typically are, though throughout my working life I have wanted to make the world a better place. And I still want to make the world a better place, earn respect, and silence my father's reproaches, although he died more than a decade before I wrote this book.

I share a fragment of my story here because work is so personal. For many of us, our first waking thoughts turn to work. On a typical day, our main activity is work, whether paid or unpaid, ongoing or episodic. At work we earn food and shelter. Through work we find mentors and become mentors to others. At work we have the ability to promote or to damage the common good. And our history constantly shapes our efforts.

Our work shapes and defines us. Europeans laugh at the American tendency to ask people about their occupation, but it makes sense since work both forms and reveals the spirit. Whatever our job, it leads us to acquire certain skills and mindsets. Scripture often identifies people by their work. Matthew called Pilate "the governor," and Jesus called Nicodemus "the teacher of Israel" (Matt. 27:2; John 3:10). David is "the king," Nathan "the prophet," Lydia "a seller of purple goods," and Luke "the beloved physician" (1 Chron. 29:9; 2 Sam. 7:2; Acts 16:14; Col. 4:14). Jesus is "the carpenter" and "the prophet" (Mark 6:3; Matt. 21:11). Of course, we are *more* than our occupations. If a journalist is also a father, mountain climber, juggler, jazz pianist, chess player, and prison volunteer, we miss the man if we stop at *journalist*.

So work is personal, but it is social too. Whatever our skills, our community shapes the work itself and the way we experience it. The status of an occupation varies from one time and place to another. The esteem and compensation given to farmers, physicians, drivers, teachers, salespeople, entertainers, carpenters, pastors, domestic laborers, and engineers rise and fall according to the social needs and economic perspectives of each era. Like living things, occupations are born, they mature, and they die. Today we have software designers and cosmetologists; in past decades we had ice cutters and town criers. Muscle power, once so vital, is dwindling in importance while mental and emotional skills are surging in value. Even when occupations endure, they change. In colonial days, almost 90 percent of Americans farmed, either part-time or exclusively. Farm families had an array of skills that are now performed by specialists. Today only 2 percent of North Americans are farmers because crop yields have increased so sharply in recent years.[1] Farmers now need expertise in finance and equipment, since machines plant, fertilize, and harvest food. Machines even milk and inseminate cows. In its use of advanced technology, farming is typical of many sectors of the economy. Manufacturing and production jobs constantly move toward automation and specialization because this increases productivity. Artificial intelligence is on the horizon and promises to increase the rate of change and reward those with the skill or flexibility to adapt to it. Yet it threatens workers who resist adaptation. These shifting trends constantly alter life for both individuals and society. Though machines deliver us from backbreaking toil, they also eliminate the need for physical skills.

---

1. "Occupational Outlook Handbook: Farmers, Ranchers, and Other Agricultural Managers," April 13, 2018, United States Department of Labor, Bureau of Labor Statistics, https://www.bls.gov/ooh/management/farmers-ranchers-and-other-agricultural-managers.htm.

Economic and technological trends consistently reshape work. We dismiss dystopian fiction, in which a dilapidated humanity falls to the machines it created, but that fiction sells because it engages real fears. Employers constantly demand new skills from their workers, and many try to squeeze ever more output from full-time employees. At the same time, the number of freelance laborers keeps growing. The sheer variety of names for the part-time worker's economy—the gig economy, the peer economy, the platform economy—suggests a field in flux. Whether by choice or by necessity, in 2017, 36 percent of American workers earned a living on an on-demand or contingent basis, and the percentage is rising steadily.[2] They cater meals; drive vehicles; wait tables; consult with businesses; repair, clean, and share homes; and care for pets. They write everything from manuals to scripts to computer code in the effort to string together income. In the gig economy, workers gain both freedom and uncertainty, since they never know when the next income-producing task will appear.

Physically, we spend more time sitting and talking than we did in ages past. Epidemic rates of obesity and diabetes reflect the decline in physical toil. Research and technology are opening exciting vistas for inventors and designers. But rising stress levels in medicine, technology, finance, and the military are alarming. Meanwhile, onerous tasks remain. People still trap rats, collect garbage, wash floors, enforce the law, and comply with government regulations. Recent changes make it all the more important to know the enduring biblical principles for work.

A Definition of Work

To think clearly about work, we need to define it. David Miller labels work as "human activity that has both intrinsic and extrinsic value; that involves physical and emotional energy;

---

2. Stephane Kasriel, "Four Predictions for the Future of Work," December 5, 2017, World Economic Forum, https://www.weforum.org/agenda/2017/12/predictions-for-freelance-work-education.

that can be both tedious and exhilarating; and that often is done out of necessity and in exchange for financial remuneration but also is done out of joy and in return for self-fulfillment and accomplishment." Miller knows that work can be drudgery or delight, voluntary or mandatory, meaningful or meaningless, satisfying or soul-crushing. Miller finally defines work as "a sustained exercise of strength and skill that overcomes obstacles to produce or accomplish something."[3] Miller rightly observes that work requires *sustained* action. One needs a willingness to suffer in order to finish arduous tasks. By Miller's definition, *work* is also broader than *employment*. The employed get material compensation in return for time, energy, and skill spent on assigned tasks. But unpaid labor, whether preparing food, tending children, mowing grass, or helping refugees, is work too.[4]

Work and *Good* Work

This book will study work, but it especially aims to promote *good* work. Years ago, scholars distinguished the *being* and the *well-being* of great institutions like marriage, civil authority, and work. In that spirit, I interviewed dozens of people, asking, "Do you like your work? If so, why?" I hoped to locate common themes and to promote faithful, constructive, and rewarding labor. Drawing on Scripture, the vast literature on work, and interviews, I propose that *good* work has five elements: need, talent, disciplined effort, direction, and correct social appraisal. We will begin with need.

Good work *meets real needs*. It provides food, clothing, shelter, education, and medical care. Historically, most people tilled fields and tended animals to feed and clothe themselves. Good work also lets people flourish through education, invention,

---

3. David Miller, *God at Work: The History and Promise of the Faith at Work Movement* (New York: Oxford University Press, 2007), 19.

4. An activity like childcare clarifies the connection between work and paid employment. Parents work when changing a diaper as surely as childcare workers do. If both parties meet the same need, they both work, whether they receive payment or not.

communication, entertainment, and the arts. When laborers meet needs, they love their neighbors, near and far. Buildings, musical instruments, and furniture can last for centuries, so quality work produces an enduring product and lets us serve neighbors not yet born.

Talent is the ability to acquire meaningful skills quickly. The boy who runs faster than anyone else at school is talented. So is the boy who remembers whatever he hears. Scripture calls talents "gifts" because they are God-given (Rom. 12:3–8; 1 Peter 4:10). People say they like work that challenges them and helps them transform their talents into mature skills.

Effort and *discipline* enter when a gifted runner meets a coach who tells him what his speed could accomplish on a soccer field. Will he strive to become a champion? Discipline is also seen when a boy finds that he can remember as he *chooses* and then chooses wisely. As a young man, John Calvin had a prodigious memory. He honed his gift by spending time each night reviewing the reading of the day and fixing the essentials in his mind. It served him well.

Direction is essential too. Years ago, a prime minister compared capable people to battleships. Engineers design warships to project power as instruments of state. Their structure is set, but their direction is essential.[5] Do the authorities direct captains to conquer defenseless people or to protect their borders? In World War II, Adolf Hitler and Winston Churchill both had great rhetorical talent and persuaded their people to fight for a cause. But they had opposite *directions*. Hitler stirred resentment to motivate conquest of peaceful neighboring nations. Churchill roused Britain to defend itself.

Finally, for work to flourish, it needs *the right social appraisal*. Society continually appraises work in a market economy. To stay in business, companies need to make a profit. If no one wants to buy their products and services at a price that is profitable for the

---

5. Chapter 9 develops the theme of structure and direction.

company, perhaps the company's work is inferior. But markets err too; great music and technology can languish undiscovered. Even on a strictly economic level, social appraisal can be faulty. Faulty appraisal causes other problems as well. In market economies citizens pay attention to products that sell, to companies that make a profit, and to jobs that pay well, whether they are constructive or not. At present, the United States pays its best athletes and actors up to one thousand times more than its teachers. Superb athletes and entertainers can earn $500,000 per week, while superb elementary schoolteachers may earn $500,000 per decade. Market economies devalue common skills, however important they are. It's hard to change pay scales, but we can at least *see* the men and women who clean floors and tables. After all, if all garbage collectors and politicians disappeared simultaneously, whom would society miss first? Market economies especially devalue volunteer labor, since no money changes hands. Stay-at-home parents and volunteers do essential work, whether paid or not. We should honor work that meets needs and promotes justice and mercy.

"All Work Is Equal"—Truth or Rhetoric?

Christian authors like to say all labor has equal dignity. They rightly question the old distinction between sacred and secular work and affirm that all honest labor pleases God. To wash dishes, clothes, and floors is to serve God. God blesses mechanics, farmers, and preachers alike, if they fulfill their callings. Important as these points are, they are not the *whole* truth. In our zeal to motivate individual workers, we act like cheerleaders, shouting, "Your work matters! It lasts forever, whatever you do." But motivational cheering neglects vital distinctions. In fact, some work neither lasts long nor matters much. Promotional items, for example, can be so flimsy that they are essentially debris—why make them?

The statement "All work matters" invites the motivational but imprecise thought that stock clerks matter as much as executives.

As a human being, everyone matters equally, but at work, those who lead have more impact. When I asked people, "Do you like your job?" many answers began with, "I do because my boss . . ." A godly kitchen hand is God's light in the restaurant, but the chef shapes the entire kitchen's structure and culture, making it a joyful or stressful place for all. I once worked on a four-man maintenance crew in which everyone was injured within three months. Why? Because antiquated equipment and hot liquids were everywhere, and the boss didn't protect his people. Unemployment was high. If one man quit, replacements lined up at the boss's door. The maintenance crew was disposable. Because the head of maintenance permitted a workplace filled with dangers and void of safeguards, the crew's efforts to avoid injury were doomed. In this sense, the work of the leader mattered the most. True leaders create healthy work environments. That includes the provision of proper equipment.

So the saying "All work is equal" is true from one perspective, but empty rhetoric from another. All work is equal in that a stock clerk and an executive can *please God* equally. And every honest job has equal dignity. But an executive shapes a company, and even society, in a way that a stock clerk never will, and it's ludicrous to pretend otherwise. As a former pastor and a former stock boy, I'm sure I did more good with a strong sermon for a thousand people than I did when I put olives in the most convenient spot for a low-ranking cook.

Jesus said, "Everyone to whom much was given, of him much will be required, and from him to whom they entrusted much, they will demand the more" (Luke 12:48). Great gifts bring great responsibilities. If the Lord has given you the skill and opportunity to lead, seize it and do good (Gal. 6:10; Eph. 5:17). Beyond that, talented leaders attract bold people. When David, so skilled in music and war, had to flee from a deranged King Saul, hundreds of men rallied to his side. Dozens eventually became "mighty men" (2 Sam. 23:8–39). So, yes, all work is important, but leadership is more important.

Justice, Social Reform, and Work

This leads us to ask if a believer is free to take any job, provided it's legal. First, we need to define *legal*. For centuries, gladiatorial "games" and animal fighting were legal and popular with a certain crowd. We cringe to think that men fought each other to the death or that people trained dogs to kill bulls, bears, and other dogs for sport. But which occupations will seem loathsome in a century? Gambling? Boxing? Football, with all its concussions? Might lawyers excoriate the adversarial system in a century? Might industry spurn the burning of oil, gas, and coal?

Gambling is a good test case, since it's legal and widespread. On one level, we can say work is good if it allows workers to do justice to their neighbors, near and far. To press deeper, work is good, first, if it is moral. Second, work is good if it builds character and evil if it wounds character. Third, toil is good if it achieves good goals but evil if it is aimless or harmful. Fourth, work is good if it pleases God, conforms to the structures of his world, and fits his vision of the good.

Let's apply these tests to the gambling industry. To some, gambling seems like harmless entertainment or even a social good, since state lotteries fund education. Others call it theft, since it takes a person's money without offering a good or service (except diversion). Winners deprive neighbors of their money, and losers deprive themselves or their families. Gambling debases character by encouraging people to take money without offering anything in return. It achieves no noble goals; it preys on the poor, and it fosters addiction. It shatters the families of chronic gamblers and contradicts God's order by exalting chance and offering wealth without labor or planning. Therefore, believers should not work in the gambling industry, even if they have a knack for it. One can be *skilled* at boxing and gambling, but that doesn't make boxing and gambling *good* work.

Here are questions we can use to appraise our work: Does my job advance the common good? Do I help people or exploit them? Am I glad to tell people what I do? Do I please the Lord as I earn my bread, or do I merely earn my bread? Can I joyfully present my work to the Lord? If we can't answer these questions properly and with a clear conscience, we should probably seek different work. Or, if we have the right position, we could try to reform our organization. To say it another way: too much Christian instruction on work urges disciples to be faithful in the work assigned to them. Not enough consider, "Should we do this work?"

Leaders should ask themselves: Is the work I oversee good? Should it be redesigned, strengthened, or even abolished? This book often calls for *reform*, but there are products and activities that should be eliminated, not restructured. So much labor goes to tasks that are pointless, even destructive by most measures. This holds true in obvious cases, like gambling, pornography, or cigarette production. But should we produce food that is high in calories and barely nutritious, even if demand for it stays strong? Should we devote talent and energy to creating violent video games that are calibrated to addict their players? Some work is perfectly legal but utterly immoral. I am *not* asking that we outlaw potato chips, but I am asking whether disciples should devote their lives to marketing potato chips.

By questioning marginal labor, we guard an important principle: to do good work, we need more than skill, persistence, and good motives; we must do good to "the other," who receives our efforts. Labor has effects in the external world. All acts have social consequences; therefore disciples must ask, "Does my work contribute to the common good?"[6] In short, work can be skillful, legal, and profitable, yet dishonorable. We must focus on *both* the subjective side of work (the laborer's skills and attitude) *and* the objective aspect (the results of the toil). So the statement "Whatever you do, give it your best effort" is simplistic at best and misleading at worst. Some tasks do not merit our best effort.

Thus, we *hope* to find work that demands our greatest skill

6. Josef Pieper, *The Four Cardinal Virtues: Justice* (Notre Dame, IN: University of Notre Dame Press, 1954, 1966), 59–62.

and effort. At times, evil work merits sabotage. Laborers in Hitler's munitions plants rightly botched the manufacture of war materials. Other tasks deserve benign neglect or judicious minimalism. Human energies are finite, and we should preserve them for demanding and consequential tasks. Why give our best to sweeping floors, dressing toddlers, raking leaves, or grading elementary school book reports? But other work summons our strongest efforts to sustain the good or to reform evils.

For example, the current American criminal justice system has a great need for reform.[7] The United States has the highest incarceration rates in the Western world and alarming rates of recidivism. Complicating matters, over past decades, many acts that were once civil offenses have been reclassified as felonies. Driving with a suspended license and sleeping in a library are often felonies, not misdemeanors. Therefore, even though rates of violent crime fell for decades, the legal code drives ever more criminal arrests and prosecutions. Courts could not handle the increased case load, so prosecutors, defenders, and judges began to rely on plea bargaining to settle more criminal cases.

The goal of the plea bargain is efficiency. If prosecutors believe a person is guilty of armed robbery, they make the accused an offer: Plead guilty to a lesser offense, such as illegal possession of a firearm, and get a light sentence—perhaps six months or even time served awaiting trial. Or go to trial and face the possibility of a decade in prison. In one case, a sixteen-year-old participated very marginally in an attempted robbery that ended with stitches for the restaurant manager. The teenager then faced this choice: plead guilty and get one year in prison and two years on probation, or go to trial and face possible life in prison without parole.[8]

---

7. I bypass the analysis of police misconduct. The police, lawyers, and judges should be faithful to laws regulating them, whether the criminal-judicial system needs reform or not.

8. In 2010 the case reached the Supreme Court, which judged the life-without-parole sentence that the man ultimately received (for complex reasons) to be unconstitutional.

According to Donald Dripps, a noted law professor, this system "creates incentives that induce rational, innocent people to plead guilty."[9] It is especially onerous for the poor. If the defendant is too poor to raise bail money, he will have to await trial in jail. This essentially negates the principle "innocent until proven guilty" and creates a double standard: the poor await trial in jail while the rich await trial at home.

Further, the rich can afford strong legal representation, but the poor rely on overtaxed, underpaid public defenders. With nominal representation, an innocent person will sensibly choose a year in jail, even for a crime he or she did not commit, over the possibility of a decade in prison.[10] This makes the system more efficient, but less just. For one thing, a guilty plea generates a criminal record that follows the accused for life. Worse, many convicted criminals are, in fact, innocent. In early studies, the legal community found that DNA testing exonerated *one-quarter* of convicted criminals.[11] In the plea-bargaining system, which resolves over 90 percent of all criminal cases, expediency prevails over justice. Remember the testimony of Scripture: "Woe to those . . . who acquit the guilty for a bribe, and deprive the innocent of his right!" (Isa. 5:22–23). Again, "He who justifies the wicked and he who condemns the righteous are both alike an abomination to the LORD" (Prov. 17:15). It will be most difficult to change this plea-bargaining system. May the Lord bless the lawyers and politicians who give sustained effort to reform.

---

9. Donald Dripps, "Guilt, Innocence, and Due Process in Plea Bargaining," *William and Mary Law Review* 57, 4 (2016): 1347. The entire article (pp. 1343–93), is instructive.

10. Ibid., 1363. Dripps also quotes John Gleeson, a federal judge, who says that "prosecutors routinely threaten ultraharsh, enhanced mandatory sentences that *no one*—not even the prosecutors themselves—thinks are appropriate" (ibid., 1356). See also Dan Simon, "The Limited Diagnosticity of Criminal Trials," *Vanderbilt Law Review*, 64, 1 (2011): 218.

11. Edward Connors, Thomas Lundregan, Neal Miller, and Tom McEwan, *Convicted by Juries, Exonerated by Science: Case Studies in the Use of DNA Evidence to Establish Innocence after Trial* (Washington, DC: National Institute of Justice, 1996), xix, 20, 78, https://www.ncjrs.gov/pdffiles/dnaevid.pdf.

Corporate Aspects of Work

No one can reform a nation's judicial system alone. That reminds us that a biblical ethic of work has both corporate and individual elements. Solomon says, "Two are better than one, because they have a good reward for their toil. . . . A threefold cord is not quickly broken" (Eccl. 4:9, 12). A band of allies can accomplish what no individual can. Because Western culture tilts toward individualism, we affirm the corporate or communal thrust of Israel's law as it touches work. Biblical narratives quietly make this point by juxtaposing descriptions of godless societies and Israel. At Babel, humanity unites in rebellion against God (Gen. 11). In Genesis 12:2–3, God counters by calling Abraham and promising, "I will make of you a great nation . . . and in you all the families of the earth shall be blessed." In Genesis 18–19, God calls Abraham's household to do "righteousness and justice," in contrast with Sodom, a city marked by lusts and violence (18:19–20; 19:4–5). So ethics is a social concern and "not simply a compendium of moral teaching to enable . . . individuals to lead privately upright lives."[12] When we read Scripture, we should ask both "What does this require of me?" and "How does it shape our community?"

Cain's question, "Am I my brother's keeper?" (Gen. 4:9) sounds reasonable to an individualist but not to an Israelite, because the people *did* keep each other. Consider this law: "When you build a new house, you shall make a parapet for your roof, that you may not bring the guilt of blood upon your house, if anyone should fall from it" (Deut. 22:8). Because Israelites worked, entertained, and slept on their roofs, it made sense to build retaining walls—parapets—around them. In the heat this kept Joshua, that reckless child, or Aunt Abishag, an overactive sleeper, from tumbling off the roof. It prevented the "guilt of blood."

---

12. Christopher J. H. Wright, *Old Testament Ethics for the People of God* (Downers Grove, IL: InterVarsity, 2004), 48–51.

An individualist wants to claim, "I would never fall off a roof. Why should I build walls to safeguard fools?" The law in Deuteronomy, however, says fools *are* our responsibility. If they fall off our roofs, *we* are guilty because we didn't protect our neighbor. Justice and mercy are core values for societies as well as individuals (Matt. 23:23; Mic. 6:8). A just and merciful city protects people who are reckless enough to pitch off a roof.

We may think, "I would never fall from a roof," but everyone has self-destructive tendencies. Without God's help, we all destroy ourselves. But God loves people who fall off buildings. The command to put up parapets is a biblical principle. It means that God chooses to protect fools and addicts, liars and thieves. God's love for self-damaging people led Jesus to his work: the work of redemption. That redemption is the foundation for all that follows, and we are right to believe that it renews our work as it renews our soul.

God-Centered Work

The topic of work is complex, so it is best to state the fundamental biblical principles before proceeding. First, I want to ground all work in the person and work of the triune God. Second, I enumerate twelve principles that guide this project.

First, then, we are creative because the Creator made mankind in his image. Certainly, no human can create *ex nihilo* ("out of nothing"), as God did, but we can create in a secondary sense by reshaping existing materials. Of course, since mankind is rational and relational, our creativity touches more than physical materials. Second, our desire to mend the broken, improve the insufficient, and optimize the inefficient echoes God's resolve to redeem his broken world. Third, our drive to make plans and accomplish them echoes the God who planned and accomplished redemption. Like the Son, we can embrace great projects and say, "My food is to do the will of him who sent me and to accomplish his work" (John 4:34). When we complete our work, we may even exult "It is finished," as Jesus did (19:30). Fourth, the Spirit renews us in the image of Christ (Rom. 8:29), so that believers are Christomorphic—formed by Christ and reshaped to become more like him.

If our life is indeed Christomorphic, we may expect to complete our work with the sweat of our brow and with the blood of suffering, for Jesus' work brought him unique anguish. As with Jesus, our efforts to reverse the results of sin will elicit resistance. Workers who are intent on reforming work must be willing to suffer for their cause, as Jesus did. With these God-centered principles in hand, we can list the first principles for a biblical theology of work. Most will be familiar, but stating our twelve foundational principles from the outset seems right. Every chapter assumes and develops the following principles:

1. **God works and ordains that humans work.** The Lord created heaven and earth and sustains his creation daily (Gen. 1:1–2:4; Isa. 45:18; Col. 1:16–17). Because God made us in his image, we can express creativity as we develop, sustain, and protect his world. Furthermore, since God chose to work and commissioned Adam and Eve to work before they rebelled, we should not view labor as a burden. Various forms of work are difficult, but in itself, work is good (Gen. 1:26; 2:15).

2. **The Lord worked six days and rested one, setting both a pattern and a limit for humanity.** The Lord said, "Six days you shall labor and do all your work, but the seventh day is a Sabbath. . . . On it you shall not do any work" (Ex. 20:9–10). The Lord both works and rests. His pattern leads away from two common errors: ceaseless toil and laziness. He corrects both workaholics and sluggards. He says "Mankind must work" and also "People must stop working." There is more to humanity than toil. Like God, we work, rest, and reflect. The law instructs the faithful to work six days, then rest, but after Jesus'

resurrection, the week begins with a celebration of redemption and rest.

3. By working with his hands, Jesus showed that all honest labor is noble. By performing manual labor, Jesus honored shepherds, farmers, carpenters, servants, and everyone else who uses muscle power. When Paul commanded believers to work with their hands (Eph. 4:28), he ennobled manual labor, which Greek society typically scorned. Today, technological devices minimize manual labor. Machines dig ditches and assemble automobiles. An array of power tools make contruction and repair vastly easier. Nevertheless, the Lord respects both mental and physical labor.

4. Mankind's rebellion led God to curse the ground. As a result, work became toil and frustration. Today, thorns and thistles blight human labor. Disorder and entropy afflict creation. Sin mars all our activity (Gen. 3:17; Rom. 8:18–23). Since Babel, all communication is fraught with misunderstanding (Gen. 11:1–9). Even the best job has jarring and painful moments.

5. Labor is mandatory for survival. The earth does not dispense food or clothing to those who put forth no effort. We must work to live. Therefore, "If a man will not work he shall not eat" (2 Thess. 3:10), and "Anyone who does not provide for his family is worse than an unbeliever" (1 Tim. 5:8). We lose sight of this since many individuals, especially the sick, the young, and the old, may not work. Collectively, we must toil. This reminds us that work has individual and corporate aspects. Our work ethic cannot merely attend to individual experience. The world is complex. People must work together to survive, and collaboration changes us.

6. Work shapes human identity. People called Jesus "the carpenter" (Mark 6:3). When Scripture identifies people as priests, fishermen, soldiers, merchants, or tax

collectors, it acknowledges the link between work and identity. Through our work we shape the world, but our work also shapes us. It leads us to gain certain skills and to see the world in light of our skills and experiences. Nonetheless, God primarily establishes human identity by making man in his image and adopting believers into his family.

7. Work and vocation are not identical. Jesus worked with wood and stone, and Paul made tents, but they had other God-given callings. Men and women can temporarily labor in a field while moving toward a position that better fits their gifts and interests. Vocation entails service in the place where God has given gifts and a desire to make a difference in this world.

8. The Lord assigns places of work, yet believers can move. "Were you a slave when called?" Paul asks. "Do not be concerned about it." But Paul also tells slaves to "gain your freedom" if you can (1 Cor. 7:17–24). Therefore, we affirm a dual truth: (a) God assigns believers to specific roles or callings, and (b) he permits them to move if there is good reason.

9. Human abilities vary, and God respects them all. One's principal duty is to exercise the talents God bestows, whether many or few (Matt. 25:14–30). Steadfast labor counts; fruit matters too (Pss. 1:3; 92:14; Isa. 32:1–8; 45:8; John 15; Rom. 7:4–5). God honors what seems dishonorable and calls it indispensable (1 Cor. 12:21–26). We should exercise our most strategic gifts as far as possible. Still, each society has its notions of noble and ignoble occupations, and they may not align with God's appraisal.

10. Many human tasks are a direct result of the fall, yet no one should despise labor that mitigates the effects of sin. After all, Jesus' work of redemption "merely" reversed the effects of sin. When Jesus said "I am working" in John 5:17 after a disappointing encounter with a man he had healed, he

confessed that his ministry was toil. Likewise, our work has dignity even if we merely restrain the effects of sin. Because the Lord worked hard to accomplish redemption, we can work "heartily, as for the Lord" (Col. 3:23; Eph. 6:5–9), even on tasks that follow the fall. Garbage collection, pest extermination, and care for the terminally ill are therefore dignified.

11. God calls every disciple to full-time service. We deny that some work is sacred and some secular. Faithful farmers, manufacturers, engineers, teachers, homemakers, and drivers please God as surely as faithful pastors do. As long as their work is honest, disciples can always pray "Thy kingdom come" as they work (Matt. 6:10, 33).

12. In our work, we can become the hands of God. When we ask for daily bread, God grants it through farmers, bakers, and grocers. When we pray for clothing and shelter, he gives it through shepherds, cotton farmers, and construction workers. Human service often goes unseen (Matt. 25:31–46). Toil is often invisible, like the stage crew and business managers behind the actors in a play. Here too, we detect an echo of God's work, since the Spirit's work is often unseen.

Discussion Questions

1. Describe your work. What tasks do you perform for pay? What do you do in your home and in your community?

2. Describe the example your parents, mentors, and significant peers set regarding how you should or should not work? What did you learn from their strengths? Their weaknesses? Have you let either one shape you too much?

3. Do you work too hard? Not enough? What would your friends say about the way you work?

4. How has your work shaped you or even defined you? Do you like the way it has shaped you? Why or why not?

5. Do you believe all work is equal? In what sense is the cheer "Your work matters" true and important? How can it be misleading?
6. How does the work of God the Creator and Jesus the Redeemer shape you as a whole? As a worker?

2

THE GLORY AND THE
MISERY OF WORK

One day a renowned developer with an oversized ego visited a luxurious golf community late in its construction phase. The plan proposed an elegant clubhouse in a hollow, circled by lavish homes, crowned by a flag atop a hundred-foot pole. The developer was on site as the pole lay on the ground. He glanced at it and shouted, "That's six inches too long!" The project manager took offense. "It is *not*. I supervised this myself." The developer retorted, "OK, let's bet on it. If I'm wrong, I'll double your price. If you're wrong, you do this for free." The engineer took the bet, measured the pole, and groaned; it measured a hundred feet and six inches. Behold the glory and misery of work: the glory in glancing at a huge steel tube and knowing its length, and the misery in using that knowledge to harm another person.

A biblical theology of work will account for this juxtaposition of grandeur and misery, nobility and vexation, at work. To look ahead, the next two chapters will gather the biblical teaching on the dignity and brokenness of work under four categories: creation, rebellion, redemption, and restoration. This four-part theology of work will serve as the foundation for later, more practical, chapters. We begin with a survey of God's original intentions for work.

Work at Creation

In the Beginning, There Was Work

One Sunday, when I led a large church, I preached four times, hosted one meeting over lunch, and hosted another meeting after evening worship. After the last event, someone who knew my schedule whispered, "You must be exhausted." I replied, "Tired, not exhausted. I loved all of it." It is a blessing to relish one's labor, to tire oneself in a beloved task (Prov. 8:30–31; Eccl. 2:10, 24–25).

God ordained work from the beginning, so we know it is intrinsically good (Gen. 1:26–2:15). Scripture blesses all sorts of vocations and mentions, favorably, the work of shepherds, farmers, kings, tentmakers, carpenters, servants, physicians, and more. God respects both manual and mental labor, leaders and followers, so that whatever we do, we can "work heartily, as for the Lord" (Col. 3:23). The root of hearty labor lies in the work of God himself.

The Work of God the Creator

In most religions, the gods do not work. In ancient Near Eastern religions, the gods did not create the world. At most, their activities accidentally brought it into being. The gods of Greece didn't create either. Aristotle's god was an unmoved mover—pure thought dwelling in celestial isolation. In Epicurean philosophy, god probably made the world, but abandoned it ages ago. In Greco-Roman myths, the gods laze about Mount Olympus most of the time.

The true Lord, by contrast, is a master builder who designs and sustains creation. When he finished his work, he took pleasure in it and declared it "very good" (Gen. 1:31; Prov. 8:22–31).[1] Even after the ravages of the fall, this world is the work of his hand (Ps. 102:25; Heb. 11:10). The heavens still proclaim his skill,

---

1. In Proverbs 8, Wisdom is both God's companion in creation and one who delights in his work. When we read from a New Testament perspective, we see that Wisdom is a personification of Jesus. This means the triune God collaborated in the joyful work of creation, since the Spirit is named in Genesis 1:2.

in earth and sky, in sounds and colors, in plants and animals (Pss. 19; 104). If the heavens are "the work of [his] fingers," mankind is the crown of creation (Ps. 8:3, 5–8). He governs mankind (Acts 17:25–26), but his people are his first concern and he offers to bless their labors (Deut. 2:7; 14:29; 16:15).

God is a king, which is a job, not just a title. He is a *good* shepherd (Ps. 23) and a warrior who defends Israel (Ex. 15:3; Isa. 42:13). He is a gardener, watering his plants (Ps. 104:10–22), a farmer planting a vineyard (Isa. 5), and a potter working his clay (Jer. 18).

God speaks metaphorically when he states, "My hands . . . stretched out the heavens," but Jesus *literally* worked with his hands, first as a carpenter, then as a healer (Isa. 45:12; Mark 6:3–5; 8:23). *Carpenter* translates *tekton*, which means one who builds or fabricates with wood, stone, or metal. Thus, Jesus was an artisan. Early Christians reported that Jesus and Joseph made yokes and plows. By working with his hands, Jesus dignified all who earn their bread manually. Since Jesus also worked long hours as Teacher, Savior, and Redeemer, he encourages knowledge workers too (Mark 4:38; 5:35; 9:17). Using secular categories, we might say Jesus had two careers, first as a skilled laborer, then as a public intellectual and spiritual leader. By his example, Jesus elevated both physical and intellectual work, so-called blue-collar and white-collar labor.

The Work of Jesus the Redeemer

Jesus' exertions as prophet, healer, and teacher exhausted him (Matt. 8:23–27), but they also satisfied him, as Isaiah foretold (Isa. 53:11). John 4 describes a day when Jesus is weary. His disciples bring him food and encourage him to eat, but he says, "My food is to do the will of him who sent me and to finish his work" (John 4:6, 31–34 NIV). Jesus found work nourishing too, and he gladly worked until exhausted. At best, work summons our highest gifts and stretches our limits. When absorbed in work, clocks dissolve, mealtimes pass, and we hardly know where we are. The best work does not deplete our energy; it renews it. Jesus knew the experience. As he died on the cross, he exulted, "It is finished," and then delivered his spirit to the Father (19:30). "It is finished" *can* refer to Jesus' substitutionary atonement, but the phrase normally means just that—something is finished. Jesus finished his redemptive task by laying down his life. When Jesus says, "My food is to do the will of him who sent me," he means that his work invigorates him. Since Jesus is the archetypal human being, we might be able to experience similar results.

To call a leader "task oriented" is typically meant as a criticism, since it suggests he lacks interest in people, but Jesus demonstrates both dedication to people and dedication to tasks. He finishes the *task* of redemption, giving his life as a ransom, because he loves his *people* (Matt. 20:28). We can at least partially imitate Jesus in his passion for both tasks and people.

Working in God's Image

God created mankind in his image, and because he works, he designed mankind to work. If we fail to work, we wither. Certain people choose to go years without working much. Some live on royalties from past efforts; others draw on an inheritance, a benefactor, or a prosperous spouse. A life of leisure may seem pleasing, but those who are idle miss opportunities for growth. They will also see their skills atrophy as they miss the soul-forging crucible of work. Others suffer unemployment due to injury, disability, or changes in the economy. They may experience anxiety or depression because they have lost the sense of purpose that accompanies work.

In Genesis 1–2, God blesses mankind and commands us to work. God calls work a blessing and issues five commands that explain one another. Mankind, made in God's image, must "be fruitful and multiply and fill the earth and subdue it, and have dominion" over the animals (1:28). The terms *subdue* and *dominion* do not encourage exploitation of creation, for God soon charges Adam to "work" and "keep" (ESV) or "tend and watch over" (NLT) the garden of Eden (2:15).[2] Genesis teaches mankind to be stewards, rulers, and guardians of the garden, and then of the wider world beyond. This leads to an array of tasks—growing food, caring for children, building civilizations. When creation was formless, God shaped it, and when it was empty, he filled it. Like God did, we should be fruitful and fill the earth. His command entails more than procreation. Animals reproduce by instinct, but humans usually have children by design, with plans for the future. Similarly, God creates life by design. He *planned* to give life, and we can too. To fill the earth is also to form culture and civilization. The command to "subdue" suggests that the world will resist. To form a culture demands a "real assertion of will," even before the fall.[3]

Ideally, we work as God works. He governs, plans, and splashes colors onto his cosmic canvas. We can't create from nothing, as he does. Still, God also operated with given material when he fashioned man from dust and woman from a rib (Gen. 2:7, 22). That encourages our world-shaping labor. Further, when God tells Adam to name the animals, he introduces classification and science. Beyond that, God designs and appoints humans to serve as vice-regents who govern his creation.

As we pull weeds and plant seeds, we realize the world's potential for beauty. As we develop our minds and bodies, we make them instruments of righteousness (Rom. 6:12). At work and at home, we should strive to oversee God's world as he would. He placed vast potential in this world; it is our privilege to bring those riches to fruition. But after the fall, the dream of realizing the world's potential seems ludicrous. Dead-end jobs, failed marriages, and lingering illnesses crush our hopes. Embittered, we scoff at optimists. When we hear of governing the world for God, we think, "I can hardly manage my desktop. Make my *mind* an

---

2. The verb *abad*, translated as "work" or "tend," has a range of meanings, including ordinary work, forced labor, and service to God. *Shamar*, translated "keep" or "take care," means to watch or guard, often for the sake of others.

3. Tim Keller, *Every Good Endeavor* (New York: Penguin, 2012), 45.

instrument for God's rule? I can barely sit still to read a serious book for twenty minutes. Make my *body* an instrument for God's rule? I just learned that onion dip doesn't count as a vegetable."

Although grand ideals may invite derision, hope exists for work, even after the fall. We will shift to the miseries of work shortly, but first we must consider the ongoing strengths of work despite human sin, for God restrains the effects of sin, even after the fall, so that his favor remains on large swaths of work. We can still accomplish vital tasks, expect a return for labor, and gain skills. We see tasks accomplished when Israel returns from the Babylonian exile and overcomes opposition to rebuild Jerusalem's walls and temple (Ezra 4–6; Neh. 2–6). Nehemiah said the wall went up because "the people had a mind to work" (Neh. 4:6). The wall also went up because God answered prayer (6:9–16).

The book of Proverbs also affirms that labor is fruitful despite sin. Proverbs seems to assert that *anyone*, even an unbeliever, can accomplish much if they have skill and determination. Still, Bruce Waltke demonstrates that the perspective of Proverbs is covenantal. To find genuine success, people must fear the Lord and commit their way to him (Prov. 1:7; 9:10; 16:1–4). In that context, keen observation reveals God's order and "the deed-destiny nexus"—the connection between actions and results.[4] Working *outside* a covenantal perspective, Ecclesiastes concludes that toil is vanity and so wretched that death can seem appealing (2:4–23; 4:2–6). Since all is vanity without faith, the best one can do is sip the transient pleasures of food, drink, and sleep (2:24–26; 5:12). But Proverbs says that faithful workers should expect a return for their labor; because God oversees the world, the diligent normally prosper:

- "A slack hand causes poverty, but the hand of the diligent makes rich" (10:4; cf. 21:5).

---

4. Bruce Waltke, *The Book of Proverbs: Chapters 1–15* (Grand Rapids: Eerdmans, 2004), 1:50–55.

- "The hand of the diligent will rule. . . . He will get precious wealth" (12:24, 27).
- "In all toil there is profit, but mere talk tends only to poverty" (14:23).
- Do you see a man skillful in his work? He will stand before kings" (22:29).

Proverbs 10 further develops this theme. It begins, "A wise son makes a glad father" (v. 1), and adds, "Treasures gained by wickedness do not profit, but righteousness delivers from death" (v. 2). Moreover, "The Lord does not let the righteous go hungry," but God "thwarts the craving of the wicked" (v. 3). The righteous work hard *and* have friends in the hour of need, so their desires "will be granted" (v. 24; cf. 18:24).

Is this always true? Aren't there times when the righteous suffer and the wicked prosper? Don't the righteous become unemployed due to forces outside their control? Yes, there are exceptions, but virtue and wealth normally travel together: again, "A slack hand causes poverty, but the hand of the diligent makes rich" (Prov. 10:4). In time, the diligent "will rule" (12:24; cf. 12:27).[5] A slack hand is negligent, sluggish, but the diligent person is thoughtful, attentive, and resolute. He earns wealth that lasts, while the idle "suffer hunger" (19:15). Timeliness is essential. "He who gathers in summer is a prudent son," but the son who slumbers during the harvest "brings shame" (10:5). Joseph personified the wise son who brings joy to his father when he seized the opportunity to deliver his family. When he worked to avoid famine in Israel, he blessed both his family and the people of Egypt (Gen. 37–50).

At work we serve God and neighbor, but we also benefit personally when we challenge ourselves and hone our skills. Hebrews 5:14 (NIV) highlights the importance of training:

---

5. Proverbs uses different terms for the word *hand*. The slack hand runs from wrist to fingertip. If you couldn't even work that much of your body, you would have been doomed to poverty. The diligent hand stretches from elbow to fingertip.

"Solid food is for the mature, who by constant use have trained themselves to distinguish good from evil." Similarly, Paul tells Timothy to "fan into flame the gift of God." This happens when Timothy preaches the faith, whatever the cost (2 Tim. 1:6–14; 4:1–5).

Intense effort pays off even for work that isn't strictly necessary. Basketball aficionados may recall game six of the 2013 NBA finals. The San Antonio Spurs led the series against the Miami Heat, 3–2; the Spurs also led game six, 95–92, with fifteen seconds to play. Miami had the ball and needed three points to tie the game and stay alive in the championship. LeBron James, then the Heat's star, missed an open shot, but a teammate grabbed the rebound. As he got the ball, Ray Allen backpedaled to the corner of the court, ready for a pass. He had no easy task. He had to sprint backward, *without looking*, to the narrow space between the three-point line and the out-of-bounds line. Allen got the ball and, with an opponent dashing toward him, launched a shot as time expired. If he missed, his team lost the championship.

Allen had practiced for this moment for years. Day after day, Allen would lie on the floor on his back, then pop up and run to the three-point line, without looking, and hit shot after shot. In fact, he said he deliberately put his body "in precarious positions coming from different parts of the floor."

In real time, Allen's shot looked impossible. His legs scissored strangely and he landed awkwardly, but he said he felt good. "I gave myself a great chance to make that shot. It wasn't unfamiliar to me, positionally. Once I got my legs there, I just let the ball go." The shot went in, which tied the game; the Heat won in overtime and captured the championship days later. Allen's creative, relentless practice was an essential reason for their win.

Sports offer a glimpse of glory and misery at work. Competition brings out the best and worst in us. It demands excellence, but if athletes or coaches care too much about winning, they may be tempted to bend rules, cheat, or demonize rivals. The same shift from healthy competition to rivalry can befall any walk of life, from musicians to inventors, scientists, surgeons, and even pastors.

The Misery of Work

Since the fall, work can be painful in at least four ways: (1) the fall brings misery; (2) personal and corporate sin create misery; (3) human follies cause misery; and (4) social factors complicate the misery. Despite all this, we have reasons to hope.

The Fall Brings Misery

The fall led to various forms of misery at work. Because of human laziness and lust for profit, engineers ignore design flaws, manufacturers cut corners, and marketers lie about their goods. Cars manufactured on Monday morning suffer from workers' hangovers, and cars manufactured on Friday afternoon suffer from the haste of laborers hurrying to leave. A selfish landlord, with inside knowledge that a road closure will stifle nearby retail business for a year, will still rent out retail space to naive clients, knowing it may ruin them. We hardly need to mention ordinary sins such as gossip, moodiness, sandbagging, grasping credit for success, and shifting blame for failure. To these failings humans add greed, deceit, pride, laziness, selfishness, and a critical spirit.

After mankind's rebellion, God cursed the ground, so that creation itself thwarts our efforts. Work became toil (Gen. 3:17–19). Drought, hail, and pests ruin crops; disease kills livestock; and extremes of heat, cold, and rain damage equipment. The world endures genetic decay and mutating diseases.

Vast amounts of labor simply try to mitigate or reverse the effects of sin. Without the fall, surgeons, soldiers, policemen, insurance agents, counselors, exterminators, dentists, and prison guards would all be unnecessary. Besides, our best efforts founder on entropy. Everything falls apart, so that work is frustrating (Rom. 8:18–23).

The fall hampers work, even apart from sin. Automakers can sin, as one company did for years, when it systematically produced false emissions tests for its vehicles. But an automaker can have noble intentions and still commit to designs that cause cars and trucks to burst into flames or crash. Errors that cause distress are evil, but not necessarily sinful. (All sin is evil, but not all evils are sins.)

The fall also blinds us to our weaknesses. Misjudging our gifts, we pour energy into the wrong projects or obsess about jobs that neither are nor should be ours. In *The Plague*, Albert Camus captures this in his character Joseph Grand, a city clerk and aspiring writer. He dreams that his novel will unfold flawlessly if he can just write the perfect opening sentence. Grand scribbled hundreds of versions of a pedestrian sentence about a woman riding a mare, making tiny adjustments each time. But Grand discovered his purpose in life by accident, when he battled the plague that ravaged his city. Although sin and the fall blind us, we can hope that God will awaken and redirect us.

Personal and Corporate Sin Create Misery

A biblical survey of work-related sins begins in Genesis 11. At the tower of Babel, people devoted themselves to a godless construction project. They hoped to "make a name for [them]selves, lest [they] be dispersed over ... the whole earth," even though God commanded that they *should* disperse themselves (11:4–9; 1:28).

Babel was the first of many forms of corporate evil. The American institution of slavery represented another form of *systemic* evil—that is, even if a given master was kind, slavery lends itself to abuses. For example, a benevolent master might die and leave his slaves defenseless.[6] The late European slave trade manifested systemic problems too. While kidnapping, shattered

---

6. We can also distinguish societies where a few individuals had slaves from societies where slaves seemed essential to the social fabric (i.e., slave societies). Slave societies have more slaves and adamantly resist change.

families, and the abuses of Southern plantations capture our attention, the way captains transported potentially mutinous slaves is often forgotten. Survivors endured unspeakable pains, but worse, perhaps a million people died in transit. The work was so odious that slave traders often had to kidnap men to crew their ships. Sadly, slave traders, human traffickers, and others do "work" that is evil from conception to completion.

God gave the law and sent his prophets to restrain sin at work. The law forbids theft, abuse of property, and failure to pay wages (Ex. 20:15; 22:1–15, 22–23; Deut. 24:14–15). It penalizes fraud, in ancient forms: moving property markers and using false weights and measures (Deut. 19:14; 25:13–16).[7] Many lands feature a vast disparity between rich and poor, but God's law ordained means to mitigate inequality. It forbade the accumulation of property by stipulating that land sold in any fifty-year period returned to the family that owned it at the start of the half century (Lev. 25). It prohibited interest on loans to the poor (Ex. 22:25; Deut. 23:19). The law also protected servants by granting them time to rest (Ex. 20:10). It prescribed punishments for abusive masters (21:20–21, 26–27), and required the release of slaves within six years (21:1–6). Farmers were also instructed to leave grain at the edge of their fields for gleaners (Lev. 23:22; Ruth 2).

Unfortunately, it is doubtful that Israel *obeyed* these good laws. Although it violated God's will, Solomon put his own people through forced labor for his grandiose projects (1 Sam. 8:17; 1 Kings 5:13–16). So we can see that the very existence of these laws is a testimony to the sins they prohibit.

The prophets cried "woe" to the rich, for their greed wounded the poor. They also hurt themselves. As the rich built imposing houses surrounded by acres of land, they squeezed out ordinary people and doomed themselves to isolation (Isa. 3:14–15; 5:8–9; Amos 4:1; 6:4–7; Mic. 3:2–3).

7. Christopher J. H. Wright, *Old Testament Ethics for the People of God* (Downers Grove, IL: InterVarsity, 2004), 76–211.

Biblical Wisdom Laughs at the Human Follies That Create Misery at Work

If the Law and the Prophets forbid *sinful* work, the Wisdom Literature invites us to laugh at *foolish* work.[8] Even ants know to gather food during the harvest, but the sluggard lies on his bed when there is work at hand. How long will he sleep? Just a little longer. Solomon concludes, "Poverty will come upon you like a robber [or wanderer], and want like an armed man" (Prov. 6:6–11; cf. 10:5). There is a distinction here. Poverty may *wander* into the sluggard's life like a vagabond, steal what it can, and move on, or it may barge in like a brigand. Laziness can bring *occasional scarcity* or *permanent poverty*. Sluggards may taste want lightly and sporadically or with terrible force.

Many sins have both light and heavy forms. Sluggards are like reckless drivers. One day the car lurches off the road. The driver assesses the damage: "Not too bad. I need to be more careful, but I'm OK." But bad habits can gain an iron grip. Eventually the car is smashed and the driver is in the hospital.

Meanwhile, the sluggard flops on his warm bed like a door turns on its hinges. He claims, "There is a lion in the road," as if to venture outside is to invite death. When he finally rises, he "buries his hand in the dish" and is too derelict to bring it to his mouth (Prov. 19:24; 26:12–16). The sluggard would be humorous if his life were not so tragic. He is too "wise in his own eyes" to heed counsel, but God's order stands. "The sluggard craves and gets nothing" (13:4). Paul agrees: no labor, no food (2 Thess. 3:10).

Laziness has a contrary sin. Solomon describes overwork through clusters of "counter-proverbs." They stand side-by-side and juxtapose apparently contrary ideas. Solomon begins, "Do you see a man skillful in his work? He will stand before kings"

---

8. I knew a man who was a fighter pilot and successful lawyer before he became a best-selling novelist. Every conceivable publisher rejected his first novel, which was about aerial combat in World War II. As he waited for the final rejection letters from marginal publishers to dribble in, he told me that he started working on a sequel. This was also rejected. However, because his third novel was a hit, he could laugh at himself.

(Prov. 22:29). Talented laborers may even *dine* with kings, but the counter-proverb warns, "Put a knife to your throat" lest you devour his delicacies and earn his displeasure (23:1–3). So the reward for excellence has complications. Solomon continues, "Do not wear yourself out to get rich; do not trust your own cleverness" (23:4 NIV). Or "Do not toil to acquire wealth; be discerning enough to desist" (23:4 ESV). Why? Because wealth flies from our hands (23:5).

So why exhaust yourself? Why not pause and rest? There are reasons: Low pay forces many to take two or three jobs just to survive.[9] Yet many professionals *choose* overwork.

When I first studied Proverbs 23, I was working seventy-five to eighty hours per week and losing weight because I could not find time to eat. I had just been with a group of large-church pastors, many of whom had health issues. They had worked to exhaustion for years, and their bodies were betraying them. Even spiritual leaders find it difficult to "be discerning enough to desist" (23:4). Liars, drinkers, gamblers, and overworking professionals tread similar paths. Many sins start small: a little white lie, a little too much alcohol, a minimal loss at gambling tables. Then they accelerate. Similarly, no one reaches an eighty-hour work week without first settling into a base of seventy.

Like all problems, overwork has an explanation and idols probably lurk nearby. Perhaps a critical teacher or coach sneered, "You'll never amount to anything." We may want to prove our worth, we may fear failure, or we may distrust capable subordinates. Overconfident, we think, "This has to be done right, so *I* need to do it," or "If I don't do this, no one will." Hilary of Tours is thought to have called self-important toil an "irreligious concern for God." It is impious to grind away thinking, "Without me, God's cause will fail." Overwork also serves as a distraction. It can be

---

9. The problem of low pay is complex. Global competition, low skills, and exploitation all play a role. Disciples should never exploit their employees, but not all low pay is exploitive. If a business makes no profit, it dies, so low skill almost inevitably causes low pay.

easier to solve technical financial or engineering problems than to face a difficult marriage or a wayward child.

Social Factors Complicate the Miseries of Work

Earlier I protested the cheerleading that dominates popular Christian literature about work, and I stand by that, but the ever-changing face of work has caused the uncertainties that make us yearn for cheerleaders. Joseph Schumpeter aptly called capitalism a system of "creative destruction."[10] In a capitalist or market economy, people are motivated to innovate because improved products increase sales. Further, improved processes bring lower costs, which enhances profits. So innovation brings material progress, but it also eliminates products and jobs. Occasionally it eliminates whole companies and professions. Beyond that, the market can devalue hard-won skills, so pay for those jobs plummets. No wonder people live in fear and long for encouragement.

Mechanization, notably the invention of increasingly capable and efficient robots, prompts anxiety. Innovation is believed to be intrinsically good because it promotes prosperity, but wise people try to limit its side effects. To protect inefficient jobs is the wrong approach because this eventually leads to financial ruin. To protect workers by retraining them is just and humane. Economic competition is good, but it is evil to play the social Darwinist and discard workers who happened to be employed in a declining enterprise.[11]

Specialization also drains the joys of work. Specialization

10. Joseph Schumpeter, *Capitalism, Socialism, and Democracy* (New York: Harper & Row, 1942). See also chap. 3.

11. Let me refine this point slightly. In business, profits generally rise when costs decline. Since labor is normally a business's principal cost, managers can increase profits by increasing productivity, reducing wages, or cutting the workforce. This makes pay cuts and job loss an ongoing threat. The number of manufacturing jobs in the West has been declining for decades. Everyone wonders what robots will eliminate next. Will humans stop evaluating loans, driving vehicles, diagnosing diseases, teaching classes? Resilient people retrain for new tasks, but others despair. Meanwhile, loyalty between workers and employers erodes, and that demoralizes workers too.

thwarts the normal human desire to see the results of our labor. God himself delighted when he gazed on his creation, and Jesus longed to see the fruit of his suffering. Since God created us in his image, we also long to see the fruit of our labor. Before the industrial revolution, farmers milked cows and drank that milk the same day. They ate the vegetables they grew and the animals they slaughtered, and there was satisfaction in that.

Mechanization and specialization both reduce costs. Machines increase productivity and wealth because they work rapidly, in heat, cold, light, and dark and never rest. So mechanization drives displacement. With *specialization*, people become more efficient by performing the same task, which is often a mere sliver of a manufacturing process. Specialization increases speed and accuracy, but it can press people to work at a pace dictated by machines or computer algorithms that are not attuned to human beings. Indeed, people doing specialized work often feel like machines. Specialization also hides the final product from workers. When people cannot see finished products enter the market, they may feel that they have labored in vain. Both Solomon and Paul address the fear of vain toil. Futility is central to the conclusion of Percy Shelley's poem "Ozymandias," which describes a derelict statue whose pedestal bears this inscription:

> My name is Ozymandias, King of Kings;
> Look on my Works, ye Mighty, and despair!
> Nothing beside remains. Round the decay
> Of that colossal Wreck, boundless and bare
> The lone and level sands stretch far away.[12]

We suspect that our monuments will suffer a similar fate. Indeed, if any of our work remained, we might be surprised. But we remember that work was good at the beginning. And since

---

12. Percy Shelley, "Ozymandias," in *Shelley's Poetry and Prose*, 2nd ed. (New York: Norton, 2002), 109–10.

Jesus is Lord and restorer of all, hope remains. To that hope we turn in the next chapter.

Discussion Questions

1. In many religions, the deities do not work. What effect does that have on the people who worship such "gods"?

2. We see God at work in creating the world, and we see Jesus at work as carpenter and Redeemer. How does our faith in a God who works shape our activities and attitudes?

3. Reread John 4:34 and 19:30. When do you feel that your work is food—that is, nourishing to your spirit? Do you ever exult, saying, "It is finished!"? How can we celebrate the completion of vital projects?

4. What should we learn from the way Proverbs laughs at sluggards and other foolish workers? When is it good to laugh at ourselves?

5. Reread Proverbs 22:29–23:4. Why is it important to gain singular skill at work? Why is it essential that we *not* put too much emphasis on achievement? Do *you* have enough sense to stop working?

3

THE RESTORATION OF WORK

Rebecca Green[1] has slowly restored the library at a large Christian elementary school. For fifteen years, she has curated a collection that delights and edifies her students. Naturally, she refuses to buy immoral or anti-Christian books, but she also culls inferior books that previously entered the collection. Rebecca will judge a book as substandard if it winks at immorality or uncritically adopts secular values. For example, an apparently innocent book may promote the myth that "you can do anything you want if you try hard enough." She notices when books quietly operate from a secular perspective. So books that assume that evolution can account for all animal life must go, even if they never explicitly endorse Darwinism. Rebecca assesses Christian books too. She discards volumes with inferior art, shallow characters, and preposterous plots. Rebecca's first goal is to build a diverse collection that appeals to children with varied interests, histories, and ethnicities (Rebecca is Lebanese). Therefore, her collection offers age-appropriate information while building faith and character, through books that reflect aesthetic skill. But there is more. By reading aloud in her rich, dramatic voice, she teaches students how to feel a story and read expressively. Rebecca also sees herself as a shepherd of young souls, so she recommends books that match student interests and abilities.

---

1. This story is based on a personal interview. Names and some details have been changed.

Still, Rebecca's restoration is imperfect. Like most people with strong ideals and high standards, she can get frustrated with parents and administrators who (incredibly) don't embrace her vision. And a naive donation of inferior books can trigger a minor crisis. Rebecca reads them and laments, "How could they think I'd let *those* books into *my* library?" But the head of school knows that these donors give funds, not just books, and it would be unwise to offend them. Alas, the pursuit of excellence is never simple, even for a children's library. Still, Rebecca has advanced her school's mission by restoring its library. And she loves it. In her words, "I love to introduce books to kids, to open new worlds to them *and* to their parents. I also love my coworkers, my community. We have a great school. If money were no object and no one complained, I'd do it for free."

The restoration of work spells both a return to God's original intentions and a measure of relief from the miseries of sin. Hebrews teaches that restoration is *real but partial* in this age. Hebrews quotes Psalm 8, where David asks, "What is man that you are mindful of him? . . . [You] crowned him with glory and honor. You made him ruler over the works of your hands, putting everything in subjection under his feet" (Heb. 2:7–9; Ps. 8:4–6). Yet Hebrews adds, "At present, we do not yet see everything in subjection to him" (2:8). Let us highlight the words *not yet*. Those two words both admit that we never rule perfectly in this age and promise that we *will* rule one day. Today we glimpse and sample the grandeur of work as God intended. By his preserving grace, the value of labor never disappears, but Scripture never promises that the redeemed will achieve all that they desire.

For believers, faith in the triune God is the foundation for the restoration of work. *The Father both commands us to work and empowers our efforts.* He gave mankind skills and opportunities to work. *Union with the Son redirects our work.* Ephesians teaches that anyone who has "learned Christ" has "put on the new self" (4:20–24). Thieves no longer steal; rather, they work so they "have something to share" with the needy (4:28). Christ also renews relationships. Servants "obey [their] earthly masters . . . with a sincere heart," knowing that God will repay them, even if their masters do not (6:5–8). And masters must treat their servants well, remembering that even lords have a Lord and Judge (6:9). *Work is also Spirit empowered.* The Spirit enabled skilled workers to build the temple (Ex. 28:3; 31:3; 35:31) and kings to rule well (1 Sam. 16:1–13). In the new covenant, the Spirit bestows gifts so believers can use them for "the common good" of the church (Rom. 12:3–8; 1 Cor. 12:7–11). The Lord also gives unbelievers the ability to work productively.

The Lord both renews us for our work and directs us in our works. He directs us in two ways: through Scripture and by granting wisdom to understand and develop his creation. Later chapters will discuss this further. Here we will consider how to read Scripture to guide our work. Naive Christians think Scripture focuses on law, as if God chiefly guides believers by giving commands to follow. In fact, Scripture directs believers in four ways: (1) by leading us toward good *goals*, (2) through laws that state God's *standards* for work, (3) through instruction on the core traits of godly *character*, (4) and through *discernment*, so we can distinguish evil from good and good from best. This discussion will begin with goals, then move to laws, character, and discernment.[2]

Good Goals—The Cure for Vanity

Workers often fear that they labor in vain, and rightly so. Fine art fades into oblivion, great inventions fail for lack of proper marketing or manufacturing, and sterling policy proposals never gain a hearing. Despair tempts us when we have noble goals but fail, or fear we will fail, to achieve them.

Job *assumes* he works for naught and asks why (9:29). Solomon

---

2. I develop these "four ways" at length in Daniel M. Doriani, *Putting the Truth to Work* (Phillipsburg, NJ: P&R Publishing, 2001), 97–157.

repeatedly laments the problem of vain labor (Eccl. 1–2; Ps. 127:1–2). Paul often fears that he labors in vain (Gal. 2:2; 1 Thess. 2:1; 3:5), especially when sees his churches falter (Gal. 3:4; 4:11; Phil. 2:16). Still, the apostle assures believers that their labor is not ultimately pointless: "Therefore, my beloved brothers, be steadfast, immovable, always abounding in the work of the Lord, knowing that in the Lord your labor is not in vain" (1 Cor. 15:58; cf. vv. 2, 10, 14).

We know that faith drives out despair, but how does it operate? First, faith gives us worthy goals. Second, faith assures us that our work is fruitful, even if we never see the results.

Consider Johannes Gutenberg, the inventor of the printing press and movable type. He aimed to reproduce texts at reduced costs, in sufficient quantities to grant common people access to great texts, beginning with the Bible. Essentially bankrupted by his effort to print the Bible, Gutenberg died in near obscurity, probably thinking that he had labored in vain. But others saw his project to fruition. His invention fueled the Renaissance, the Reformation, the development of modern science, and the movement toward universal literacy. Not bad as legacies go.

Gutenberg's story shows that good work may have unseen results. Because they believed in his cause, dozens of people supported Gutenberg. Skilled workers taught him metal-working, benefactors funded his project, and visionaries promoted its potential. Gutenberg's history encourages us to persevere and take a long view of our work, which often seems futile, if viewed myopically. Humans simply cannot detect the results of their efforts.

Conversely, workers may think their work is vain because it *is* vain. To produce and market cigarettes and the worst junk food *is* to labor in vain. If we suspect that our products are inferior, we should pause and reflect.

The "God at Work" movement, which has encouraged people to practice their faith in their places of work, rightly emphasizes motivations for work. It assures believers that their work matters, that they can dedicate it to God. That said, *motivation and dedication are necessary but not sufficient conditions for worthwhile labor.* It is false to state that God is pleased with whatever we do, provided that it is dedicated to him and not immoral. We must have the right goals and achieve them the right way. Truly good work uses the right means, has godly motivations, and pursues beneficial goals. Good work is both lawful and helpful to humanity.

To illustrate this, let's turn a classic "your work matters" story on its head. One day a traveler came upon three stonemasons at work. He asked each man what he was doing. The first replied, "I am cutting stones." The second said, "I am earning my living." The third answered, "I am building a cathedral to the glory of God." The lesson, allegedly, is obvious. Masons do more than cut stones and earn money, they glorify God by building cathedrals.

Or do they? Does a mason glorify God because he *intends* to glorify God? In fact, an act pleases the Lord when it meets three criteria: (1) The *goal* must be a desire to glorify God, (2) the *standard* must be God's law, and (3) the *motive* must be love for God and neighbor. It is doubtful that cathedrals meet these criteria. By what biblical warrant did medieval leaders devote vast human and material resources to those buildings? Although God instructs Israel to build a tabernacle and endorses the temple, he doesn't give an imperative to construct grand church buildings. Scripture does, however, command generosity to the poor. It took 263 years to erect the Strasbourg Cathedral. The Notre Dame of Paris took 185 years. Both required thousands of tons of stone. It took the wood of 5,000 trees just to construct the roof of Notre Dame. And how many laborers died in construction accidents? Large-scale building projects almost always result in fatal accidents, and the height of cathedrals must be considered. Poverty was widespread through much of the cathedral-building era, so perhaps medieval Christians should have built homes and hospitals instead. Eventually people *did* question the most grandiose project, St. Peter's Basilica. Indeed, its stupendous costs and later abuses in raising money became a catalyst for the Reformation.[3]

I concede that cathedrals provide lasting places for worship, that their soaring arches and windows can lead to thoughts of transcendence, and that it is not fitting to belittle the motives of the pious. Still, strong motivations for ill-advised projects bring more harm than good. It is not sufficient to assert that our work glorifies God. A truly good act follows God's laws, conforms to his character, and has proper goals. To choose goals correctly, we must weigh the results of our activity, lest an effort to please God wound humans instead. Cathedrals deserve scrutiny on that point.

Workers must have worthwhile goals. Is space exploration worth the cost? Is needlepoint worth the time? What shall we say of colonialism, which brought the benefits and diseases of the West to Africa and the Americas? When does the church's missional impulse cause harm by fostering dependence?[4] In short, rightly motivated people choose the right projects and implement them in the right way. We need wisdom to assess the culture's notions of good projects—cathedrals, conquest of other lands—and choose goals that fit God's law and reflect his character. This points us toward God's standards for work.

Good Standards—Applying God's Law

One of the great problems at work is immoral behavior. A former car salesman told me he resigned when his supervisor said, "I don't care if you have to lie, cheat, or steal. Sell more cars." Sadly, every industry has its temptations to lie, cheat, and steal. To counter that, God gave his people laws that teach them how

---

3. The need to fund St. Peter's led to an extraordinary effort to sell indulgences. For a substantial fee, one could buy documents declaring release from all temporal consequences of sin, in this life or in the alleged millennia of purgatory. Many objected; Luther's protest, grounded in the gospel, caught fire.

4. Steve Corbett and Brian Fikkert, *When Helping Hurts* (Chicago: Moody Press, 2009, 2012).

to keep their way pure (Ps. 119:1–16). To study the laws for work, we will begin with the Decalogue.

Commandments 1–3

Work becomes a demigod if we turn to it for identity and security. The commands to love God, forsake other gods, and make no images imply that work should not take too much space in our hearts. And since believers bear the name of Christ, the command, "You shall not take the name of the LORD your God in vain" (Ex. 20:7), reminds us that everything we do brings him honor or shame. In all our work, we strive to bring credit to God's name.

Commandment 4

Every law reflects God's character. We protect life because God is the life giver, we tell the truth because God does, and we rest because God rests. The fourth commandment, "Remember the Sabbath day, to keep it holy" (Ex. 20:8), is rooted in God's nature. When he created the universe, he lavished vast skills on it, yet held something back. He detached from his work enough to pause and evaluate it. By stepping back, God showed that his work neither defines nor exhausts him. There is more to God than his work, and there should be more to us too. God says, "Stop working endlessly. Rest, worship, play, relax with friends. To do these things is to live by faith, to trust me, the Father, to provide, even as you rest." The godly do not think, "I must provide for myself; no one else will."

Commandment 5

"Honor your father and your mother" (Ex. 20:12) teaches us to respect supervisors and mentors at work, since Scripture calls various leaders "father" (2 Kings 2:12; 5:13). Imagine the transformation if workers honored their leaders more and criticized and complained less. What if, upon hearing a questionable directive, we thought, "What can I learn from this?" or "I wonder what I'm missing?" rather than, "What an idiot."

Commandment 6

"You shall not murder" (Ex. 20:13) teaches believers to promote life in our realms of work. The obligation is clear in medicine, but we can protect life in every sector of the economy. Builders, architects, engineers, metallurgists, firefighters, drivers, soldiers, and parents all guard life by working safely and creating safe products.

Commandment 7

"You shall not commit adultery" (Ex. 20:14) requires disciples to be faithful at work. Faithfulness forbids the plots, duplicity, and broken promises that spoil the workplace.

Commandments 8–9

"You shall not steal" (Ex. 20:15) forbids both direct theft of money and materials and the indirect theft that infiltrates work in other forms: dishonest advertising, cheating on quality control, overcharging naive customers, and enrolling clients for services they don't need. "You shall not bear false witness" (Ex. 20:16) applies here too, for dishonesty is foundational to many forms of economic injustice, including theft.

Commandment 10

Greed drives numerous sins in the workplace. "You shall not covet" (Ex. 20:17) forbids the love of possessions that drives us to overcharge, overwork, or take the wrong job simply because it offers wealth or power. Better to work, trust God to provide, and believe that "godliness with contentment is great gain" (1 Tim. 6:6; cf. Ps. 37:16; Heb. 13:5).

Scripture has relatively few specific rules for work. God trusts his people, guided by his Spirit, to apply the Decalogue to their work situations across the ages. This fits the pattern of Scripture, which also has few specific rules for parenting, marriage, finances, and similar topics. After all, the Bible is the story of redemption, not a legal code. Besides, most of today's jobs didn't exist centuries ago. Still, Scripture has a few concrete rules. Some call on common sense: Builders must make structures safe (Deut. 22:8). Farmers work hard at the harvest (Prov. 6; 26). Shepherds should guard their flocks (Ezek. 34; Luke 15:3–7).[5] Rulers and judges will punish evil and do justice (Ex. 18:21; 23:8; Deut. 16:19; 27:25; Mic. 7:3; Rom. 13:1–7). These points seem clear, but when temptations come, what was once clear can begin to look murky.

The Bible seems to assume that there is a way to do all work well, even if that work is somewhat unpleasant.[6] To find the right path, workers may need wise counsel and discernment to resist the temptations that beset all vocations. For example, recall that rulers and judges must do justice. But the rich try to bribe judges so the judges will *not* be impartial. Likewise, courtiers may urge the king to enjoy the wealth and pleasures of office (cf. Deut. 17:14–20). Similarly, when repentant tax collectors and soldiers asked John the Baptist what to do in Luke 3:10–14, John let them stay in their profession but told them to resist the temptations unique to their work. Specifically, tax collectors should "collect no more than" authorized, and soldiers should not threaten but should "be content" with their wages (Luke 3:12–14). Both can stay in their occupations if they avoid the abuses common to them. Similarly, Joseph and Daniel kept working for pagan kings.[7]

Every vocation, even the most respected, has its temptations. Teachers can dominate their students; physicians can bloat with pride. In our quest to be godly workers, we must read Scripture carefully, pray, and examine ourselves.[8] But again, God does not

---

5. Theologians sometimes call these principles *natural law* since nature itself teaches farmers to bring in their crops and shepherds to care for their animals.

6. Immoral "professions" like thievery and prostitution are forbidden.

7. In an extreme case, we see that Elisha let Naaman, chief military commander of Syria's armies and a new convert, go with his king "into the house of Rimmon," Syria's deity. Since Naaman knows he will need to "bow" there, he asks for mercy in advance; Elisha replies, "Go in peace" (2 Kings 5:15–19). Chapter 6 explores serving in difficult positions, including serving pagan kings.

8. See chap. 9.

give laws for every occasion. We need wisdom. Even more, godly character is a compass that teaches us to navigate the landscape of work. If a ruler has Christlike character, for example, he will refrain from using his position to serve himself, for Jesus used his position to serve others, not himself. This will be our next theme.

Godly Character: Love, Justice, and Faithfulness at Work

Character is foundational, since it is "the chief architect of our actions and decisions."[9] If people know what they *ought* to do, character gives the strength to do it. Character brings the right dispositions to moral situations, and that is vital when there are no rules in sight.[10] To possess character is to have a compass and to believe that a proper compass matters because discernment of right and wrong matters. People of character love good and hate evil, and they pursue the good, even under duress.

Biblical teaching on character begins with love: "You shall love the Lord your God with all your heart," and "You shall love your neighbor as yourself" (Matt. 22:37, 39). The Decalogue largely teaches us how to love: We love our neighbor by protecting their family, their property, their reputation, and more.

Scripture highlights justice and faithfulness as well as love. God's revelation of his character in Exodus 34:6–7 names all three: "The LORD, the LORD, a God merciful and gracious, slow to anger, and abounding in steadfast love and faithfulness, keeping steadfast love for thousands, forgiving iniquity and transgression and sin, but who will by no means clear the guilty." The word *faithfulness* appears explicitly, and it is implicit in the mention of steadfastness. Because God is just, he does not clear the guilty. Love is also named twice, and grace is a form of love. Jesus endorses this view when he refers to "justice and mercy and faithfulness" as "the weightier matters of the law" (Matt. 23:23).

---

9. Bruce Birch and Larry Rasmussen, *Bible and Ethics in the Christian Life* (Minneapolis: Augsburg Fortress, 1989), 81.

10. Doriani, *Putting the Truth to Work*, 105–10.

We may begin with *love*. Jack Cottrell defines God's love as "his self-giving affection for his image-bearing creatures and his unselfish concern for their well-being that leads him to act on their behalf."[11] The same points—affection, concern, and action—will be visible in human love. Second, *justice* gives everyone their due, as God defines what is due.[12] Justice includes equality before the law and fairness in all interactions. In that vein, Paul says, "Pay to all what is owed to them" (Rom. 13:7). Third, *faithfulness* is endurance in all virtues, including love and justice, and in all proper commitments.

Justice without love is harsh, and love without justice is indulgent. Faithfulness is also essential because no character trait has weight if it manifests itself sporadically. When love and justice meet in our work, we can find direction even in the hardest decisions.

Consider the Christian business leader who doubts the importance of love at work. Love cannot be measured on a financial statement. How does it enhance production, marketing, distribution, or labor negotiations? The improvement of faltering employees? Love sounds like a disposition, but business leaders want measurable outcomes. They can't afford sentimentalism. They need to dismiss pleasant but incompetent workers, and they need to close inefficient operations.

Can a Christian manager be loving *and* fire people? Absolutely. To be sure, dismissals seem unloving, but love is more than being nice to people. Partnered with justice, love could *require* layoffs. A biblical ethic of work has both individual and corporate

---

11. Jack Cottrell, *What the Bible Says about God the Redeemer* (Joplin, MO: College Press, 1987), 336.

12. John Frame, *Systematic Theology: An Introduction to Christian Belief* (Phillipsburg, NJ: P&R Publishing, 2013), 258, 66. In *The Republic*, Plato says that to do justice is to render to each person what is due, but in Plato's view "what is due" is an ideal or form that exists apart from God. In *A Theory of Justice*, John Rawls takes justice to mean that everyone has the same basic rights and duties and "the most extensive basic liberty compatible with a similar liberty for others" (John Rawls, *A Theory of Justice* [1971; repr., Cambridge, MA: Belknap, 1999], 14–15). That is a splendid concept of justice from the perspective of human rights, duties, and happiness.

angles. If a worker is flailing at his or her job, a reprimand is an act of love if it comes with respect and counsel for improvement. If that employee fails to improve, termination may be necessary, even loving. How so?

First, to *keep* feckless employees is unloving to all who must cover their mistakes and do their jobs for them. Indeed, in a competitive economy, a firm can collapse if inept workers stay indefinitely. Besides, failed workers normally know the truth and feel miserable. They probably have gifts that can be used elsewhere and may need the jolt of dismissal to overcome whatever drives their poor performance. So it *is* loving to correct and coach struggling workers, and eventually to dismiss them (with dignity) if necessary. However, it seems neither loving nor just to dismiss skilled, productive workers for marginal increases in profits.

Christianity stands alone in calling love the prime motive for action.[13] The Bible endorses many motives—duty, anger at injustice, a fear of displeasing someone—and all have a role in our daily actions. But love has primacy. If a business excels in its field and earns solid profits, its people probably act in love at many points. They love clients by using their skills to meet their needs. Workers love their supervisors and coworkers by fashioning a good environment for work. Bidding and negotiations are loving if they are honest and give the other party what it most needs whenever possible. When a company earns an honest profit through good products and service, everyone prospers, from investors to employees to customers.

The union of love and justice brings out the best in workers. Teachers of all kinds join love and justice when they both affirm their students and demand that they do their best. Civil servants do their best when love for the community leads them to practice justice.

Once, after a college football game, I witnessed a case in

13. Charles Taylor, *A Secular Age* (Cambridge, MA: Harvard University Press, 2007), 112–15.

point. I was walking from the stadium with a large crowd that was heading back to campus or toward far-flung parking lots. We came to a large intersection where three roads met. A traffic cop was directing cars and pedestrians with skill and enthusiasm. He waved long lines of vehicles through the intersection as pedestrians stacked up behind him. When he judged the crowd to be large enough, he whistled all cars to stop and then gestured grandly that we could cross however we pleased. One inebriated driver decided to drift through the intersection with the throng. He crept along at first, then moved faster through the crowd, barely missing several walkers. The officer blasted his whistle, but the car kept going; he sprinted toward the accelerating vehicle and grabbed the door handle. The car rolled on, with the policeman dashing alongside. Suddenly, he swiveled and unleashed a tremendous kick, putting a large dent in the driver's door. The driver stopped, rolled down his window and shouted, "Hey what are you doing to my car?" The policeman grabbed him by the shirt, yanked him halfway out of the window, and told him exactly what he was doing, in a speech that was equal parts eloquent and irate. When the officer stopped, the crowd burst into applause. The officer demonstrated both love and justice. His passion for justice led him to accost a scoundrel, but he also loved the people and the work itself. His expertise and passion, his act of love and justice, led the crowd to spontaneous applause.

Discernment: The Pragmatist, the Witness, and the Prince

We have studied the role of proper goals, God's law, and godly character in the restoration of work. One element remains: the discernment to see our work as God does and to reject secular perspectives whenever necessary. Let me suggest three metaphors that may help believers see themselves: the pragmatist, the witness, and the prince.

For the *pragmatist*, work is essentially a secular activity. The pragmatist regards family and church as sacred spaces and has high standards there. But pragmatists compartmentalize their lives and hesitate to translate biblical principles into their workplaces. They park their morals at the door and do whatever it takes to make money. At worst, pragmatists lie, falsify, steal, and manipulate, without remorse, to get ahead. Love and justice become luxuries that they consider only after profits and salaries are secure. Although misguided, pragmatists are right about this: workers do need to get results, and we may need to sacrifice to reach them. However, pragmatists fail by abandoning the proper search for ways to practice their faith and achieve their goals.

The witness emphasizes personal morality in the workplace. He or she works hard, respects everyone, operates with integrity, and tells the truth. The witness strives to show moral excellence to create a platform for sharing the faith. Evangelism is good, and a beautiful life does adorn the gospel, as the apostles teach (Titus 2:10; James 3:13; 1 Peter 3:4). Indeed, Jesus says, "Let your light shine before others, so that they may see your good works and give glory to your Father" (Matt. 5:16). That said, there can be something defective in a desire to work hard in order to gain the credibility that will later lead to opportunities to evangelize. People sniff it out when someone works for show, to prove something, instead of bending to the task itself. At worst, the witness cares only marginally for the organization and its projects.

In Nehemiah's day, the Israelites rebuilt the walls of Jerusalem despite every obstacle and foe, "for the people had a mind to work" (Neh. 4:6). The whole narrative praises that devotion to work (4:6–23; 6:1–16) even as it declares that the "work had been accomplished with the help of our God" (6:16). Similarly, Paul commands, "Whatever you do, work heartily" (Col. 3:23).[14] So we should first give ourselves to the work God assigns us. Then the opportunity to witness may follow spontaneously.

For a few months between college and graduate school, I had

---

14. Ecclesiastes 9:10 seems to make the same point when it says, "Whatever your hand finds to do, do it with your might," although there are debates about the thrust of the paragraph covering 9:7–10.

a job unloading trucks. My mentor urged me to give myself to the work. The principle stayed with me. A few years later, with my Master of Divinity in hand, I persuaded Westminster Seminary and Yale University's history department to let me create a joint program for my Ph.D. My Yale classmates were brilliant; many also had a gene that let them sit and read, uninterrupted, for eight hours. In Ph.D. seminars, there is no place to hide. Hoping to keep up with the class, I gave myself to the work. After a month studying the philosophical and religious roots of the British Civil War (1643–48) in one seminar, my professor, a famed agnostic, asked me two questions: "How do you know so much theology? And would you like to work with me?" Before long, Professor Russell and my classmates (none of them fools) deduced that I didn't just *know* Reformation theology, I *believed* it. That easily led to conversations about the faith. I propose that the order of events is essential. First, we give our talents and energy to the work, whether building roads, unloading trucks, or analyzing texts, and then we gain a hearing.

The prince also wants to be a witness. And like the pragmatist, the prince longs for results. But he also believes Jesus rules over every square inch of life and calls everyone to rule under him. Princes believe that the Lord delegates his authority to mankind and wants us to use that authority well.

Dorothy Sayers thought like a prince when she described how a Christian carpenter's faith shapes his work:

> The Church's approach to an intelligent carpenter is usually confined to exhorting him not to be drunk and disorderly in his leisure hours, and to come to church on Sundays. What the Church should be telling him is this: that the very first demand that his religion makes upon him is that he should make good tables. . . . No crooked table legs or ill-fitting drawers ever, I dare swear, came out of the carpenter's shop at Nazareth. . . . (The Church) has forgotten that the secular vocation is sacred. . . . Work must be good work before it can call itself God's work.

Christian carpenters should worship and pray, but, Sayers continues, "No piety in the worker will compensate for work that is not true to itself; for any work that is untrue to its own technique is a living lie."[15] Sayers embodied this principle in her mystery novels. Critics noted their erudition, manifest in her understanding of crime and the history of fiction. Beyond that, her characters, dialogue, and plots made her novels a pleasure to read.

Chefs, architects, builders, designers, engineers, artists, teachers, and gardeners should also strive to be true to their craft. As they consult wise men and women within their discipline, they will grow. Drivers, cleaners, and retail salespeople may have less room for creativity, but everyone should know their work and be true to it. Even a police officer can direct traffic with flair. Martin Luther King Jr. captured the idea this way: "If a man is called to be a street sweeper, he should sweep streets even as Michelangelo painted, or Beethoven composed music or Shakespeare wrote poetry. He should sweep streets so well that all the hosts of heaven and earth will pause to say: 'Here lived a great street sweeper.'"[16]

One school of thought instructs young adults to lower their aspirations and build skills slowly, tending their garden. It's sensible advice, but it sounds too modest. The world *needs* the enlightened rule of God's children. Most of the world dreams of wealth, fame, security, peace, and respect. We should aim for *more*. We are the crown of creation, and creation thrives when mankind rules wisely. We should think, "Whatever I do, I preside over a corner of God's world for him. However small that corner is, I hope to make it a better place."

15. Dorothy Sayers, *Why Work? An Address Delivered at Eastbourne, April 23rd, 1942* (London: Methuen, 1942), 15–16. This text can also be found online at http://tnl.org /wp-content/uploads/Why-Work-Dorothy-Sayers.pdf.

16. Martin Luther King Jr., "MLK Quote of the Week," The King Center, April 9, 2013, http://www.thekingcenter.org/blog/mlk-quote-week-all-labor-uplifts-humanity -has-dignity-and-importance-and-should-be-undertaken.

God's Complete Restoration

This chapter opened with a story about Rebecca, who restored her library and encountered resistance. That is inevitable in this age, but the future will be different, which may keep discouragement at bay. Counselors often urge us to let the probable future shape the present. Start saving money in your twenties, advisors say, and retirement will be easy. Care for your body in your youth, Cicero warned, because "an intemperate and indulgent youth delivers to old age a body all worn out."[17] The future of work also guides labor today. One strand of Christianity holds that praise and contemplation govern eternal life and that work and play will end. To be sure, certain *types* of work will disappear. The new creation will have no morticians, oncologists, or detectives. But Jesus apparently expects work, purged of futility, to continue in the new creation.

The parable of the talents assumes that disciples continue to work after meeting the Lord. When we meet him, he will say, "Well done, good and faithful servant. You have been faithful over a little; I will set you over much" (Matt. 25:21, 23). To be set over much sounds like *work*. In this age, leadership is an arduous, frustrating privilege. But after sin is purged by God, we may still put forth the sustained effort that is the mark of work. Even now, work is joyful when it summons our best efforts and wins us glad partners. Surely that joy can enter the new creation.

We also remember that labor is not a consequence of sin. We work because God works. When liberated from sin, labor may fit the restored creation quite well. Furthermore, the prophets imagine beautiful, perfected labor after the Lord restores all things. Amos 9:13 says, "Behold, the days are coming . . . when the plowman shall overtake the reaper and the treader of grapes him who sows the seed; the mountains shall drip sweet wine." Micah foresees a time of peace, when everyone will sit "under his vine

---

17. Cicero, *On Old Age*, cited in Luke Timothy Johnson, *The Revelatory Body* (Grand Rapids: Eerdmans, 2015), 221.

and under his fig tree" (4:4). And what reason is there to think that music, cooking, craftsmanship, engineering, art, invention, athletics, or science will end? Since we will have restored bodies and God designed bodies for action, we may expect to find pleasure in exertion, as well as in eating, drinking, and singing new songs to the Lord (Ps. 96:1). All such activities take effort and they will be blessed, if that is Lord's plan for us.

When Revelation states that "the kings of earth will bring their glory" into the New Jerusalem, we understand that the best of this age joins the next (Rev. 21:24–26). If we know that our best efforts last forever, this will motivate us to persevere in good work today. One day the Lord will halt all destructive labor. Revelation 18 describes the fiery collapse of Babylon, the city infamous for pride, immorality, and wealth. In that scene, the earth's kings and merchants stand far off, mournful yet detached, as Babylon faces its judgment. Babylon fell because it would trade *anything*, even "human souls" (Rev. 18:13). That revelation of *future* judgment warns believers to resist *today's* temptation to do anything, trade anything, if there is profit in it.

It is possible to live like a Babylonian without realizing it. Take Melissa, a kind woman who helped pay the tuition for other people's children when her income grew as a New York investment banker. She formulated the packages of debt that nearly ruined the economy in 2008–9. She said the potentially catastrophic results of her financial products "didn't occur to her," although she conceded that she should have foreseen the possibility.[18]

Consider also George, a businessperson and church elder whose chain of convenience stores sold cigarettes and pornography. When a friend learned of his business practice, he urged George to stop. George protested, "But they're so profitable." His friend replied, "Will you make money in ways that hurt your customers?" Before long, George saw that this was no way

---

18. Sheelah Kolhaktar, "Trading Down," *New York Times*, July 5, 2009.

to love his neighbors, and he stopped. Cigarettes, pornography, and deceptive financial deals all reek of Babylon. The flames are their doom. John writes, "Come out of her my, people, lest you share in her plagues" (Rev. 18:4). If we are citizens of the New Jerusalem, we need to live like it. If we are new creatures, it will show in our work.

The Bible calls God "the great king" (Pss. 47:2; 95:3; Matt. 5:35). We rule under him as vice-regents (Gen. 1–2; Ps. 8; Isa. 32:1–8). Our language reflects this when we grant royal labels, calling a man "the king of comedy" or a woman "the queen of jazz." Of course, the Lord sees excellence that we ignore. He may see the queen of the comforting family dinner that nourishes everyone there, even the unexpected guest. He knows the king of the bedtime story, the teller of tall tales that soar and then resolve in ways that gently lead children to sleep. The Lord notices our best effort washing dishes, growing vegetables in our gardens, repairing the dignity of an opponent we just crushed on the athletic field, or waiting patiently on an indecisive customer. When Jesus returns, every kind of greatness will shine for all to see (Matt. 13:43). If we believe this, we should act on it and teach it to others, so that the future keeps shaping the present.

A young pastor recently told me he grew up in a church where no one ever spoke about faith at work: "It was 'Me and Jesus,' with a focus on Sundays, Wednesdays, and overtly spiritual activities. At our church, faith had no role at work." What a sad mistake! We *can* serve God and neighbor at work. This chapter has tried to explore the role of faith in all our labor. Whether chopping onions or performing heart surgery, work is both grand and frustrating. We can call it a miserable business and endure it for a paycheck, or we can strive to glimpse the way our toil participates in God's plan to heal this world. It is a privilege to share in his purposes.

Discussion Questions

1. Why do we need God's law to guide our work? Review the Ten Commandments and state some ways the law directs the *way* you work.

2. What are your goals at work? How many of them are personal goals, such as keeping your promises or sharing your faith? How many of them focus on the work itself?

3. Why is it insufficient to *intend* to glorify God at work? Consider the masons and the cathedral. How can we intend to glorify God and yet fail to do so? How can we ensure that our work does please the Lord?

4. To what extent do you act like a pragmatist? A witness? A prince?

5. Do you agree with Sayers when she says the first task of the Christian carpenter is to make good chairs? Why or why not?

4

WORK THROUGH THE AGES

Suppose a believer wants to change her culture's approach to food. She laments rushed and tasteless meals and the way processed food, high in salt and fat and low in nutrition, contributes to obesity. She dreams of slower meals, eaten in community over conversation. She wants people to savor food and get healthier. Suppose she decides to write a book about this. An enthusiast might charge into the task, recording her thoughts, then tracking down Scriptures that support her view. The danger is syncretism—uncritically merging biblical and secular themes. We should be wary of cultural accommodation—that is, the attempt to read our culture's values into Scripture or to approve a contemporary idea by finding a verse in Scripture that seems to endorse it. If she is more careful, she might review secular literature on the topic to ensure that she has not merely duplicated familiar themes and then covered it with a veneer of Scripture.

By spending time with other cultures, we learn to question our assumptions. Otherwise, we may notice verses that endorse current perspectives and overlook those that challenge it. In a society that admires thin women (and unwittingly causes eating disorders), we should hear the man who praises his beloved by saying, "Your belly is a heap of wheat" (Song 7:2). To gain critical distance from her culture, our food writer might sample writings from other ages and lands. The same is true of work.

It is human nature to endorse our culture, especially if it works well for us. In general, whatever is common seems normal and whatever is normal seems right. So writers tend to validate their culture's values, even while advocating minor reforms, unless they become radical critics who react to everything. That principle holds true for the studies of food and work alike. If we hope to hear Scripture well, we might read perceptive secular treatises, whether they clash with God's Word or align with it. In that vein, this chapter surveys views of work through the ages, sacred or profane, especially if they shaped Christian thought and practice. Ideally, this will help us distance ourselves from "received" truths, present or past. The goal is to promote faithfulness at work.

Before we start our journey, let's remember that human and animal muscle powered most work until the twentieth century. Most people hunted, gathered, farmed, and tended herds. Until 1900, most societies were two bad harvests from starvation. Children labored alongside parents, and vacations and retirement were barely known. Meanwhile, the pace of work was steady but not frenetic.

While the shape of work changes, many questions arise repeatedly: What is the meaning of work? How much should we work? Enough to meet basic needs? More? If so, why? Should we work to avoid sloth, build character, and serve others? To develop skills or to become mature? To create time for leisure?

Is work good or evil, ennobling or debasing? Does work exalt mankind, as Renaissance humanists claimed, or does it debase mankind with beast-like toil, as the Greeks taught? Everyone agrees that work is necessary—an *instrumental* good—since toil provides food and shelter. But is work also an *intrinsic* good? Plato, Aristotle, and advocates of early retirement believe people should work as little as possible. The Greeks foisted labor on slaves. A century ago, Bertrand Russell thought technology and automation could cut the work day in half.[1] Philosophers hope

---

1. Bertrand Russell, "In Praise of Idleness," in *In Praise of Idleness and Other Essays* (London: George Allen and Unwin, 1915), 15–16.

that leisure will allow pursuit of the fine arts, friendship, and community service, but realists suspect that most people will seek passive entertainment or fall into destructive activities. Are human beings uniquely responsible to govern the world for God and steward its resources for future generations? Or is mankind one species among many, with no special privileges or responsibilities except to refrain from destroying ourselves and ruining the planet?

Should workers consciously seek the good of others? Or does the "invisible hand" of God or the marketplace redirect self-interested labor so that it contributes to the common good, as Adam Smith held? Do we help others by helping ourselves? Or does selfish action lead the powerful to exploit the weak? Is specialization constructive because it increases efficiency? Or is it destructive, since it crushes creativity by binding workers to a narrow set of tasks?[2] Specialization seems positive because it permits scientists and engineers to invent things that so improve the human condition that they quickly seem like necessities. What then is the proper view of work?

Greeks and Work

"To the Greeks work was a curse and nothing else." It was a "necessary evil" to be relegated to slaves—or artisans—if possible.[3] The Stoics resisted this consensus and respected manual labor, but Plato, Aristotle, and Epicurus found work demeaning. They held that trades and crafts were dishonorable and that laborers lived like beasts: they grew, toiled, reproduced, and died, leaving no permanent mark. Aristotle said that some people "are marked out for subjection, others for rule." Indeed, "the lower sort are by nature slaves," so that it was better for them to live "under

---

2. Miroslav Volf, *Work in the Spirit: Toward a Theology of Work* (Eugene, OR: Wipf and Stock, 1991), 58–65.

3. Adriano Tilgher, *Work: What It Has Meant to Men through the Ages* (New York: Arno Press, 1977), 3–7.

the rule of a master."[4] Thus, Aristotle reasoned, masters *assisted* slaves by ruling them. Meanwhile, slaves toiled to provide food, clothing, and shelter for their masters. Masters, liberated from irksome labor, could enjoy leisure for friendship, citizenship, and contemplation, which the Greeks considered "the activity most appropriate" for people not forced to work.[5] Aristotle's reflections on slavery conveniently ignored the case of rulers and military leaders who became slaves through defeat in battle. Marxists would argue that Aristotle's oversight illustrates the way rulers justify systems that promote their interests.

The New Testament contradicts the dominant Greek view of manual labor. After all, Jesus worked with wood and stone, Paul made tents, and Peter, Andrew, James, and John were fishermen. Among the apostles with known occupations, only Matthew, a tax collector, did no manual labor.

To put this in perspective, we recognize that pagan societies tend to imitate or create gods who endorse their values. The gods of Greek mythology were idlers, and Aristotle's god was pure thought. It is no surprise therefore that gods who do not work foster an ideology that disparages manual labor. Still, the Greeks are not wholly wrong. Unskilled manual labor can be hot, dangerous, and demeaning. Bodies break down under the demands of planting and harvesting, hauling rocks and making bricks. So we hear the Greek perspective, even if we can't endorse it.

Early Christian Views of Work

Ancient and medieval Christian concepts of work owed a debt to Greek philosophy as well as Scripture. To be sure, early church leaders knew work was necessary and praised artisans, merchants, and even soldiers, since they "contribute to the common

4. Aristotle, *Politics*, trans. Benjamin Jowett, in *The Basic Works of Aristotle*, ed. Richard McKeon (New York: Random House, 1941), 1132–33 (Book 1, chaps. 4–6).
5. Lee Hardy, *The Fabric of This World: Inquiries into Calling, Career Choice, and the Design of Human* Work (Grand Rapids: Eerdmans, 1990), 11.

good and to their neighbor's advantage."[6] Still most ancient and medieval theologians rested on the legacy of Greek philosophy and devalued ordinary work. They adopted the Greek notion that *contemplation* is the highest goal of human life. Eusebius (263–339) wrote that a higher Christian life forgoes marriage, children, and wealth, and "devotes itself to God alone." This "perfect form of the Christian life" allows "celestial beings" to pass to heaven. A "more humble, more human [life] permits men to join in pure nuptials and to produce children, to undertake government, to give orders to soldiers, . . . to have a mind for farming, for trade and the other more secular interests."[7] Augustine (354–430) said the contemplation of God is "the end [goal] of all good activities and the eternal perfection of all joys."[8] And Gregory the Great (540–604) said that "although the active life is good, the contemplative life is . . . better" because contemplation "burgeons in immortal life." A believer needs "courage of action, but contemplation brings "heavenly joy."[9]

Thomas Aquinas (1225–74), prince of medieval theologians, claimed that "the contemplation of divine truth is the goal . . . of human life," but the active life makes that difficult. For Aquinas, Luke 10 demonstrates the superiority of the contemplative life. Jesus commends Mary, who sits and listens when he visits her home, because she chooses "the best part," whereas Martha, who works hard, is troubled by many things. Aquinas admits that "necessity" may drive one into the active life, but

6. Chrysostom, "Homily LXXVII, Matthew 24:31–32," in *The Gospel of St. Matthew*, trans. George Prevost, *The Nicene and Post Nicene Fathers*, First Series (Grand Rapids: Eerdmans, 1986), 10:469.

7. Eusebius, *The Proof of the Gospel*, trans. W. J. Ferrar (New York: Macmillan, 1920), 48–49 (bk. 1:8). Most primary sources for this chapter are available online, but online translations may be inferior.

8. Augustine of Hippo, *The Trinity*, trans. Edmund Hill (Brooklyn, NY: New City Press, 1991), 76 (bk. 1:17).

9. Gregory the Great, *The Homilies of St. Gregory the Great on the Book of the Prophet Ezekiel*, trans. Theodosia Gray (Etna, CA: Center for Traditionalist Orthodox Studies, 1990), 32–35 (homily 3:4–10).

contemplation is superior because it is the best preparation for eternity.[10]

In the preamble to the charter of the Cluny monastery, William I, Duke of Aquitaine (875–918), explains why he gives funds to establish a monastery: "To all right thinkers it is clear that the providence of God has so provided for certain rich men that, by means of their transitory possessions . . . they may be able to merit everlasting rewards" by supporting monastic work. William, drawing on translations he had available, cites Proverbs 13:8, "The riches of a man are the redemption of his soul," and Luke 16:9, "I will make his poor my friends."[11] Since William had wealth, he gave "some little portion" of it "for the gain of my soul."[12] So William believes that worldly work must justify itself by giving gifts that promote contemplation.

This distinction between active or secular work and the realm of the sacred and contemplation governed Christian thought for a millennium. Everyone knew work was necessary for life. They believed that it promoted discipline and humility and prevented idleness. They held that good work or good works could contribute to salvation. Clearly, they recognized that work has *instrumental* value, but they denied that work has *intrinsic* value. Because contemplation is superior to work, a wise disciple will labor as little as possible.[13]

The Renaissance

The Renaissance promoted new concepts of God, humanity, and work. Renaissance writers were not necessarily orthodox

---

10. Thomas Aquinas, *Summa Theologica*, trans. Fathers of the English Dominican Province (New York: Benziger Brothers, 1947–48), 2:1939–45 (questions 181–82).

11. The Duke's translation of Proverbs 13:8 follows the Vulgate, but for unknown reasons, his translation of Luke 16:9 does not. The ESV reads, "The ransom of a man's life is his wealth" (Proverbs 13:8), and, "Make friends for yourselves by means of unrighteous wealth" (Luke 16:9).

12. Duke William I of Aquitaine, in *Select Historical Documents of the Middle Ages*, ed. and trans. Ernest F. Henderson (London: Bell and Sons, 1892), 329–33.

13. Tilgher, *Work*, 41–46.

Christians, but they stopped thinking of God as inactive. They said God works and humans should work too. Giovanni Pico della Mirandola's manifesto, *Oration on the Dignity of Man*, says that God gave man a creative capacity like his own. He calls God "the master builder" (or "Supreme Architect") who displayed his wisdom and power by creating the universe.[14] He says that when God created mankind, instead of giving them a fixed place, like plants, animals, or angels, God bestowed "free judgment"; that is, free choice. Thus, human beings can become their own "molder and maker," shifting downward as brutes or soaring to the "divine." Thus, we become "what we will be." Pico della Mirandola can praise contemplation, but his theology implies that the "active life" is best.[15]

Renaissance philosophers observed that human beings have hands as well as minds. Once they conceive of things, they want to make them. In this, they said, people resemble God, even if God creates out of nothing and mankind reshapes what God created. Animals build nests and webs by instinct, while human beings imitate God, "the artisan of nature," when they plan to control nature and create new things. So humanity becomes like God by creating.[16] Renaissance thinkers seemed to neglect the effects of sin, but they did recognize the craft and industry of man. The Renaissance had a mixed legacy: it ennobled human labor and subtly diminished God's role. "The notion of working *for* God had been replaced by working *like* God."[17]

Martin Luther (1483–1546)

Martin Luther famously declared that the farmer shoveling manure and the maid milking her cow please God as much as the

---

14. Giovanni Pico della Mirandola, *Oration on the Dignity of Man*, trans. Charles Glenn Wallis (1486; repr., Indianapolis: Bobbs Merrill, 1965), 4.

15. Pico della Mirandola, *Oration on the Dignity of Man*, 4–7.

16. Hardy, *Fabric of This World*, 27–28; Marsilio Ficino, *Platonica Theologica*, trans. Michael Allen (Cambridge, MA: Harvard University Press, 2004), 4:45, 49.

17. Franz Wippold, personal correspondence, March 2018.

minister preaching or praying. All honest work is holy, pleasing God, and dignified. The opportunity to do good work and good works is "present in all places, in all walks of life."[18] As we labor in our God-given stations in life, God both "conceals himself and . . . exercises dominion" through us.[19] We become "the masks of God, behind which He wants to remain concealed and do all things."[20] Luther tells farmers and milkmaids that God himself "will milk the cow through you and perform the most servile duties through you, and all . . . will be pleasing to him."[21] Thus, God milks cows through the vocation or station of the milkmaid. The pious person must believe that "hauling a wagonload of manure" is the work "God lays upon us." If not, he will get "tired of his situation" and start "staring at" others.[22] God *could* provide directly, but he chooses to hide himself behind human masks, providing food and government indirectly through our labor: "God gives every good thing, but not just by waving a hand."[23] Thus, we say that God gives wool through human labor. "If it is on the sheep, it makes no garment."[24]

Through our hands, Luther says, God answers the prayers of his children. We pray for our daily bread at night, and bakers rise in the morning to bake it, using flour that came from farmers who plant and millers who grind. By our work, the naked are clothed, the hungry are fed, and the sick are healed. By our labor, we love our neighbors. Toiling in our God-given place, we become God's agents.

18. Martin Luther, "Treatise on Good Works," trans. W. A. Lambert, in *Luther's Works* (St. Louis: Concordia, 1966), 44:98–99; Gustaf Wingren, *The Christian's Calling: Luther on Vocation*, trans. Carl Rasmussen (Edinburgh: Oliver & Bond, 1958), 9–10.

19. Martin Luther, "Exposition of Psalm 127," trans. Walther Brandt, in *Luther's Works* (St. Louis: Concordia, 1966), 45:330–31.

20. Martin Luther, "Psalm 147," trans. Edward Sittler, in *Luther's Works* (St. Louis: Concordia, 1958), 14:114; see also Luther, "Psalm 127," in *Luther's Works*, 45:331.

21. Martin Luther "Lectures on Genesis," trans. Jaroslav Pelikan, in *Luther's Works* (St. Louis: Concordia, 1970), 6:10; Wingren, *Christian's Calling*, 9–10.

22. Martin Luther, "The Sermon on the Mount," trans. Jaroslav Pelikan, in *Luther's Works* (St. Louis: Concordia, 1956), 21:266.

23. Luther, "Psalm 147," in *Luther's Works*, 14:114–15.

24. Wingren, *Christian's Calling*, 8.

Luther developed these concepts through his dispute with medieval monasticism. Priests and monks claimed the term *vocation* for religious and especially monastic work. In theory, monks had a unique opportunity to complete their faith through good works and so to gain assurance of salvation, while common laborers had no such advantage.[25] Luther countered that monastic works were vain and that assurance of salvation came by faith in Christ. Luther asserts that each Christian hears a call to believe the gospel and to serve both God and men in a station in life. Whatever someone's station may be, faith transforms it into a vocation. Every vocation is a divine commission, and all please God equally.[26] In this way, Luther begins to break down the notion that labor has two tiers, the sacred (or ecclesiastical) and the secular. This ennobles the toil of the common man.

For Luther, work is still an instrumental good, but more deeply so. Medieval theology proposed that laborers served *themselves* by earning their bread and growing in humility, but Luther looked outward. His worker served his neighbors and society, even if the work was menial or unsavory. He advised, "If you see that there is a lack of hangmen, constables, judges . . . and you find that you are qualified, you should offer your services." To exercise "governing authority" even with the sword, is to perform "divine service.[27] Thus, for Luther, the active life in society is as noble as the secluded life of monastic contemplation. Furthermore, while medieval Catholicism accented the personal benefits of work—material wealth, divine rewards, and a cure for pride—Luther viewed work as the place to serve others.

Luther's perspective proved transformative. Helpful and

---

25. Martin Luther, "The Judgment of Martin Luther on Monastic Vows," in *Luther's Works*, 44:253–316.

26. Volf, *Work in the Spirit*, 105–6.

27. Martin Luther, "Temporal Authority: To What Extent It Should Be Obeyed," trans. J. J. Schindel, in *Luther's Works* (St. Louis: Concordia, 1962), 45:95, 103; Kathy Stuart, *Defiled Trades and Social Outcasts* (Cambridge, UK: Cambridge University Press, 1999), 61.

influential as it is, it still demands assessment, beginning with his desire to dignify all human labor, however mundane and repetitive. When Luther insists that God calls everyone to a "station" as farmer or servant, he implies that each person not only *can* but *should* serve where they are. This consoles all who feel trapped by their work. How comforting it is to hear that "the menial housework of a manservant or maidservant is often more acceptable to God" than all the works of an unbelieving priest.[28] Indeed, our restless age needs the exhortation to labor in our place, instead of constantly asking, "What's next?"

But Luther's consolation has a cost. If every legitimate task is a divine call, then perhaps workers must remain in their station. If *all* lawful work is a God-given call, how can anyone seek a new position or try to reform their workplace? If all work is a divine appointment, the motive to reform unjust working conditions evaporates. Luther justifiably laments, "Everyone is bored with his way of life and sighs for someone else's." But Luther offers only one solution to boredom: "One must not think of changing his way of life but of changing his boredom." He preaches, "Cast aside . . . the boredom" and you will "realize that you neither needed nor wished a change."[29]

First Corinthians 7:20 was an essential text for Luther: "Each one should remain in the condition in which he was called." But this is half of Paul's message. Paul did say an enslaved person should "remain in the condition in which he was called" (7:20), but he also says, "If you can gain your freedom, do so" (7:21 NIV). "Stay where you are" is no absolute principle (see chap. 5). Moreover, 1 Corinthians 7:20 instructs slaves, not all workers. Slavery was all too common in the Roman Empire, and slaves were especially

28. Martin Luther, "The Babylonian Captivity of the Church," trans. A. T. W. Stein-hauser, in *Luther's Works* (St. Louis: Concordia, 1959), 36:78.

29. Martin Luther, "Gospel for St. John's Day: John 21:19–24," ed. Benjamin Mayes and James Langebartels, in *Luther's Works* (St. Louis: Concordia, 2013), 75:357–58. Luther's sermons often return to the theme of resignation to one's duty, a point discovered in the research of Vicki Tatko.

immobile. Paul helps Christians endure difficult situations like slavery, but he does *not* instruct Christians to stay in their place, even if they are free to move. On the contrary, 1 Corinthians consistently says, "Stay, unless . . ." Stay single, *unless* burning with passion (7:8–9). Stay married, *unless* an unbelieving spouse is determined to leave (7:10–15). Stay enslaved, *unless* there is opportunity for freedom (7:20–24).[30]

Luther's treatise *Whether Soldiers, Too, Can Be Saved* illumines the issue. In it, Luther uses terms such as *office*, *work*, *calling*, *occupation*, and *position* interchangeably, as if they refer to the same concept.[31] Luther seems unaware of the difference between working as a soldier and a calling to the military. But we must distinguish a temporary summons to war from a life of soldiering.

One may have an *occupation without a vocation*. One can earn bread as a cashier or nanny without being called to either task. A job pays the bills; a *calling* fits our gifts and interests. A business manager, recently laid off, may enjoy a few months as a handyman, but he sees that as a temporary job that lets him provide for his family until he returns to his calling. Jobs may even help us find our calling. While in school, I washed dishes, painted homes, unloaded trucks, and served as a teaching assistant. The first three were *jobs*; the last gave me a positive taste of my *calling*. The need to eat may require us to wash pots, but faithfulness to God's gifts may require us to leave jobs that waste our skills. Frederick Buechner says, "God calls you to the kind of work that you need most to do, and the world most needs to have done. . . . God calls you [to] the place where your deep gladness and the world's deep hunger meet."[32] Sadly, no jobs truly fulfills that concept, but Buechner does capture the ideal.

---

30. Chapter 5 explores 1 Corinthians 7 at length.

31. Martin Luther, "Whether Soldiers, Too, Can Be Saved," trans. Charles Jacobs, in *Luther's Works* (Philadelphia: Fortress, 1967), 46:94–100.

32. Frederick Buechner, *Wishful Thinking: A Theological ABC* (New York: Harper & Row, 1973), 95.

Luther's views fit adults in static societies. In his day, economies were simple and work fell into lines that seemed to follow
a natural or created order. Farmers, merchants, and magistrates
stayed in their positions for a lifetime. Moreover, these stations
were typically multigenerational; the son of a wheelwright was
apt to become a wheelwright. Luther's ideas fit less easily in
societies in constant flux. How can men and women stay in their
stations, we may ask Luther, if their stations disappear through
layoffs, restructuring, or relocation?

People love to quote Luther when he says that God milks cows
through the milkmaid. But if all honest work is a divine call or
station, how can we question dehumanizing forms of work? If
servants who cleans stalls hear Luther say it is divine work even
to lift "a straw," they will be comforted.[33] But if every task is a
divine call, who dares ask if anyone *should* perform that task, or
if current practice is the best way to accomplish it?[34]

The tendency to bless the status quo is starkly presented in
Luther's comments about slaughter in war. He wrote that "war
and killing . . . and martial law have been instituted by God."[35]
Even if some abuse the office of soldier, the validity of the office
itself remains. For Luther, God's involvement is direct: "For the
hand that wields this sword and kills with it is not man's hand, but
God's; and it is not man, but God, who hangs, tortures, beheads,
kills, and fights. All these are God's works and judgments."[36]
Luther knows that no Christian should be a thief, but he seems
blind to the way institutions and occupations can be legal and
yet disordered and in need of reform.

The summer before I entered college, I worked for a milk-
processing company that operated an in-house box-making

33. Luther, "Treatise on Good Works," in *Luther's Works*, 44:25; Volf, *Work in the
Spirit*, 106–7.

34. Volf, *Work in the Spirit*, 106–7. Volf adds, "Luther's understanding of work as
vocation is indifferent toward alienation in work."

35. Luther, "Whether Soldiers, Too, Can Be Saved," in *Luther's Works*, 46:95–97.

36. Ibid., 45:96.

machine for its specialty cheeses. One day that machine's tender was sick, and the boss appointed me as box maker for a day. I mastered the device by 10 A.M. and spent the rest of the day giving thanks that I would soon leave for college. If I could master the process in ninety minutes, should we not pity the woman who did it for twenty years? Should human beings tend machines perpetually? Luther cannot answer that question. If every *job* is a *calling*, the ability to question dehumanizing work evaporates. At worst, Luther provides justification for exploitive leaders to command pacified people to do their duties and follow orders, provided they are not wicked. Luther's teaching on work made a great contribution, but like every Reformer, he needed others to refine his insights.

John Calvin (1509–64)

Calvin agreed with Luther on most points, but he saw, as Luther did not, that sin can distort the structures of work. In Luther's day, stations of work seemed to obey a God-given order in which people generally remained within their sphere. Calvin agreed that God placed people in callings.[37] Yet he was willing to question the social order. For example, it was common in Calvin's day for theologians to condemn the behavior of abusive masters. But in his sermon on Ephesians 6:5–9, Calvin questions the *institution* of slavery. He says masters had "excessive authority . . . over their slaves" and proposes that God allowed "this state of affairs . . . because of man's wickedness." In fact, slavery is "totally against all the order of nature." It exists because Adam "perverted the order of nature."[38] These points make room for the Reformers to question and change social structures.

Calvin also considers the role of God's gifts in human callings. Like Luther, he says God has a place for each person. He

---

37. John Calvin, *Institutes of the Christian Religion*, trans. Ford Lewis Battles (Philadelphia: Westminster Press, 1961), 3.21.6 (724–25).
38. John Calvin, *Sermons on Ephesians*, trans. Arthur Golding (Carlisle, PA: Banner of Truth, 1973), 633–35.

also thinks human skill in art or science rests on the abilities God bestows.[39] For Calvin's followers, "The station is no longer itself normative." People must assess whether their labor serves God and neighbor or not. So Calvinists de-emphasize service *within* one's station and accent serving "*by* one's station."[40] If people barely serve anyone in their station, they should change stations. Thus, Calvin offers a theological rationale for mobility, and later generations develop it.

Adam Smith (1723–90)

Believers readily give thanks for the contributions of Luther and Calvin. The legacy of the Scottish economist and deist Adam Smith is more complex. Many of his principles retain a place in the concepts of a market economy, or capitalism, which most Western Christians live by and endorse. The market economy fuels the engines of innovation and efficiency and has created immense prosperity. Prosperity in turn shapes the individualistic, meritocratic outlook that assumes that one's work, income, and worth are tightly connected. Western believers tend to assume that the market economy is the best economic system. Market mechanisms enhance productivity and wealth, but Smith always saw that the drive for productivity dehumanizes workers, who are reduced to and labeled as "production costs." At worst, low-skill workers are almost commodities and their labor is acquired for the lowest possible price.

Smith proposes that productive labor is the source of wealth for nations: "The annual labour of every nation is the fund" that supplies all its necessities and conveniences.[41] For Smith, labor is a necessity, a means to create the food, shelter, pleasure,

---

39. Calvin, *Institutes*, 2.2.14–16 (273–75).

40. Hardy, *Fabric of This World*, 66–67.

41. Adam Smith, "Introduction and Plan of the Work," in *An Inquiry into the Nature and Causes of the Wealth of Nations* (New Rochelle, NY: Arlington House, 1966), lix. Smith tinkered with *Wealth of Nations*, so that the wording differs slightly from one edition to another, following the judgment of the editor, and diverging slightly from this citation. *Wealth of Nations* is also available online. See the 2017 edition by Jonathan

and security people desire. Consumption or the gratification of desire is the end or purpose of production.[42] The pleasures of labor consist in its rewards. Men want to live at ease if they can. The laborer sacrifices part "of his ease, his liberty, his happiness" to gain goods in return.[43] Smith does not meditate on the intrinsic satisfaction one may find in labor; he thinks of the instrumental value in work—the satisfaction of *desires through labor* (including the desire for a good reputation). He also knows that "masters" wish to pay employees "as little as possible," while ensuring that they at least survive, while laborers look for "an advantage," whether through a rare skill or a labor union, that will "raise their wages considerably."[44] Like Aristotle, Adam Smith believes that people want to relax, avoid toil, and, if possible, "impose [it] on other people."[45] Smith was not interested in questions such as, "Do you enjoy your work?" Enjoyment is beside the point, which is that workers use their skills to produce desirable goods. Their pay lets them obtain life's necessities and perhaps more.

Smith believes that labor and production promote the *common* good because an "invisible hand" orchestrates or harmonizes selfish human actions.[46] No one "intends to promote the public interest. . . . He intends only his own security." But to prosper, he must produce something others find useful, so he can trade it for whatever he wants.[47] By directing his efforts toward work so that it produces "the greatest value, he intends only his own gain." And yet "an invisible hand" leads him to "promote an end"—the good of neighbors and of society—"which was no part of his intention."[48] The beauty of the marketplace is that

Bennett at http://www.earlymoderntexts.com/assets/pdfs/smith1776_1.pdf.
   42. Ibid., 1:31–38, passim.
   43. Ibid., 1:34.
   44. Ibid., 1:72–75.
   45. Ibid., 1:31.
   46. Ibid., 2:29–30.
   47. Ibid., 1:13–14.
   48. Ibid., 2:29–30.

it puts human selfishness to good use. Self-interested people, seeking wealth, must produce and offer products or services with value, so other self-interested people will pay for it. Without trying to do so, selfish producers and selfish buyers do good to each other. As the economy flourishes, people have the products they want and need.

The benefits of selfishness *could* lead to harmony and prosperity, if not for the strength of the human appetite, which wants *more*. Smith argues that specialization of labor is the path to increased productivity and greater wealth. Specialization accentuates the differences between people. The highest efficiency occurs when a worker repeatedly performs simple, focused tasks, with the right tools.[49] Repetition fosters speed and efficiency. Unfortunately, repetition also crushes the soul. Thus, *the specialization that creates prosperity alienates laborers from their work*. Manufacturing also leads to the concentration of wealth so that workers have less power in disputes with employers about the speed, duration, and payment for their work. In this way, the division of labor promotes prosperity but damages the human spirit.

Karl Marx (1818–83)

If Luther's notion of calling feels static, Adam Smith's devotion to productivity seems crass and stultifying. Smith's thought has a thread of despair, since the desire for greater wealth leads to deadening work and exploitation of laborers. By contrast, Karl Marx has an optimistic view of work. Like Smith, he laments the plight of "laborers, who must sell themselves piecemeal," as if they are a "commodity."[50] He agrees that the desire for productivity will reduce "the activity of the individual worker to simple, endlessly repeated mechanical motions." Worse, manufacturers exploit workers whenever they can. Unskilled labor,

49. Ibid., 2:1–11.
50. Karl Marx and Frederick Engels, "Manifesto of the Communist Party," authorized English translation (1848; repr., New York: International Publishers, 1948), 15.

in a manufacturing environment, is a commodity. When there is an abundant supply of workers, the price for labor inevitably falls to "the minimum required for subsistence" of life.[51] In a communist society, Marx imagines, work would become a realm for self-development. In his utopian vision, no one would be limited to one branch of production and exploited by it. Everyone would explore "the entire system of production" and work "according to the needs of society or their own inclinations." Everyone would therefore put their comprehensively developed abilities to full use.[52] One wonders who would be inclined to collect garbage.

According to Marx, as humans create products and control nature, they produce themselves.[53] Bees, making honeycombs, may do better work than architects. "But what distinguishes the worst architect from the best of bees is this, that the architect builds the cell in his mind before he erects it in reality."[54] People work to survive, but Marx imagines a day when increased productivity leads to a six-hour workday, when people work freely in the arts and sciences and enjoy projects that awaken slumbering potential. Then work would become a freely chosen activity, an end in itself. In a mature communist society, no one performs stupefying tasks. All would enjoy "the free development of individualities,"[55] and unleashed human invention would create products so excellent that they would seem necessary. Agreeing with Smith, Marx says that people would serve themselves as they

51. Frederick Engels, "Principles of Communism," in *Karl Marx, Frederick Engels Collected Works*, Vol. 6: Mark and Engels, 1845–48 (New York: International Publishers, 1976), 343 (question 5).

52. Ibid., 353–54 (question 20).

53. Volf, *Work in the Spirit*, 57, 132–33.

54. Karl Marx, *Capital: A Critique of Political Economy*, trans. Samuel Moore and Edward Gaveling (Moscow: Progress Publishers, 1867, 1887, 2015), 1:127 (chap. 7).

55. Karl Marx, *Grundrisse: Foundations of the Critique of Political Economy*, trans. Martin Nicolaus (New York: Penguin, 1973), 706. Volf, *Work in the Spirit*, 59, 63–64; J. E. Elliott, "Marx's *Grundrisse*: Vision of Capitalism's Creative Destruction," in *Karl Marx's Economics: Critical Assessments*, ed. John Cunningham Wood (New York: Routledge, 1988), 286.

serve others.[56] But Marx believes labor need not be oppressive. Work requires "the most intense exertion," but when the "really free" laborer overcomes obstacles, work becomes a "liberating activity" that fosters "self-realization."[57]

Marx foundered, as many in his era did, on the absence of a concept of sin. Certainly no one successfully implemented socialism or communism. Yet the hope that Marx held for self-discovery and self-development through work still resonates. Like other Romantic thinkers of his era, Marx protested the way the market economy reduced everything to prices and profits and the way industrialization made work into drudgery. Romantics want to sense, to feel, and to become one with the world, apart from rational or scientific analysis. That goal fits nicely with Marx's desire to halt the alienation of workers from their labor.

Toward Contemporary Views of Work

The views of Adam Smith and Karl Marx have abiding significance. Adam Smith knew that specialization was the path to productivity and prosperity, but Marx countered that people hate repeated mechanical motions.

Frederick Taylor (1856–1915) pioneered fields now known as industrial engineering and scientific management. Taylor noticed woeful inefficiencies in American industries and tried to introduce precision to physical tasks such as shoveling coal. Arming his analytical mind with a stopwatch, Taylor determined that coal shovelers moved widely varying amounts of coal and ash because they adopted whatever method they pleased. Taylor found that the ideal load was 21.5 pounds and that the most efficient shovelers bent their knees, rested their elbows on their thighs, and slid their shovels along the floor. Taylor reasoned that if every laborer had the right shovel and adopted the most efficient motions, rising productivity would increase both wages

---

56. Volf, *Work in the Spirit*, 132; Marx, *Grundrisse*, 243–44.
57. Marx, *Grundrisse*, 611.

and profits. Taylor was right—and wrong. His process quickly led wages to increase over 60 percent, from $1.15 to $1.88 daily, while the cost of handling a ton of coal plummeted from 7¢ to 3¢. But there were losses. Increased efficiency meant that most shovelers lost their jobs. Remaining workers resented being treated like machines, endlessly executing the same motions.[58] In the mode of Adam Smith, Taylor stripped intelligence and problem solving from work to increase productivity. The remaining workers still had *jobs*, but they were miserable.

Job loss is one of the developments that led Joseph Schumpeter to call capitalism a system of "creative destruction."[59] In market economies, companies are motivated to innovate, since improved products tend to be profitable. Constant innovation brings material progress, but it also eliminates inefficient jobs and outdated products, creating a state of uncertainty as many people wonder how long their jobs will exist.

More recently, Peter Drucker (1909–2005), sometimes called the founder of modern management, noted dangers in the quest for efficiency: "Machines work best if they do only one task, if they do it repetitively . . . at the same speed [and] the same rhythm." Laborers don't shine at machine-like acts; they excel at perception and coordination and at bringing perception into action. They work best when "the entire person is engaged by the work."[60] Drucker foresaw that machines would replace blue-collar labor, even as he advocated respect for all laborers.

In a similar vein, Abraham Maslow asserted that once human beings meet their needs for food, clothing, shelter, safety, security, and love, they pursue higher goals—achievement and self-actualization.[61] The protest against dehumanizing work fit nicely

---

58. Hardy, *Fabric of This World*, 128–40.

59. Joseph Schumpeter, *Capitalism, Socialism, and Democracy* (New York: Harper & Row, 1942), 82–86.

60. Peter Drucker, *Management: Tasks, Responsibilities, Practices* (New York: Harper & Row, 1973), 181–84.

61. Abraham Maslow, "A Theory of Human Motivation," *Psychological Review* 50, 4 (1943): 370–96.

with his goal of self-actualization. Together they have won the day in the West. If the task is washing dishes or exterminating termites, people may admit that they work for a paycheck. But the aspiration for fulfillment and self-development is strong in Western cultures. Many adults hope for jobs that meet their needs *and* allow personal growth. Students plan to achieve this by earning degrees from prestigious colleges, cultivating relationships with mentors who guide them, heeding experts who know the path to success, and switching jobs when necessary. Cultural analyst David Brooks found that American college students believe in an orderly world:

> If you work hard, behave pleasantly, explore your interests, volunteer your time, [and] obey the codes of political correctness, . . . you will be rewarded with a wonderful ascent in the social hierarchy. You will get into Princeton and have all sorts of genuinely interesting experiences open to you. You will make a lot of money—but more important, you will be able to improve yourself.[62]

When they become professionals, Brooks proposes, these people can become "bobos," both bourgeois and bohemian. They are bourgeois because they embrace the benefits of capitalism. They are bohemian because they see themselves (probably incorrectly) as unconventional, free spirited, and dedicated to self-expression. In them, materialism and self-expression fuse. At best, there is a "higher selfishness" that includes purchases of experiences and goods that are self-cultivating. The goal is work and an income that is both fulfilling and socially constructive.[63]

To say it differently, American culture promotes two kinds of individualism: utilitarian individualists and expressive individualists. *Utilitarian individualists* are hard-working, ever-improving,

---

62. David Brooks, "The Organization Kid," *The Atlantic*, April 2001, https://www.theatlantic.com/magazine/archive/2001/04/the-organization-kid/302164.

63. David Brooks, *Bobos in Paradise* (New York: Simon & Schuster, 2000), 117–24.

self-made types, like Benjamin Franklin. They strive to accumulate wealth, power, and status. They may choose a career not because it attracts them but because it is respectable and offers material rewards. For them, happiness at work is secondary. *Expressive individualists* want a life that is "rich in experience, open to all kinds of people," and filled with "intense awareness."[64] The ideal is to claim the best of both, but most people lean one way or the other. Utilitarians work harder, cultivate relationships with superiors, and gain skills as they ascend in rank. Expressivists work less so they can go camping on the weekends. They labor not to accumulate wealth but to earn *enough* to support a satisfying lifestyle. They don't want to become a manager at their firm; they want a respectable job that ends at 5 P.M. In my interviews, one practical utilitarian expressed his mind-set this way, "I aim for mediocrity at work. When my phone rings, I may not answer it. I *don't* want people to think of me as a 'go-to' guy."

I once attended a party where a man complained that his boss had started to demand that he work up to *fifty* hours per week. Because this compromised his cycling and rock climbing hobbies, he decided to quit his job and move to a city known for accommodating people like him. The response to his story was telling. The expressivists nodded approval, but the utilitarians, who worked over fifty hours every week, rolled their eyes as if to say, "I pick up the pieces after slackers like this."

Despite their differences, both groups probably agree that work is a means to an end—happiness. Logically, almost all people would stop working if they inherited a fortune, since they work for the benefits, not because of the pleasures of work or dedication to a cause. For most, work is an instrumental good.

---

64. Robert Bellah, Richard Madsen, William M. Sullivan, Ann Swidler, and Steven M. Tipton, *Habits of the Heart: Individualism and Commitment in American Life* (Berkeley: University of California Press, 1985), 34, 291. See also 32–35, 286–96; Charles Taylor, *Sources of the Self: The Making of the Modern Identity* (Cambridge, MA: Harvard University Press, 1989), 369–76, and Charles Taylor, *A Secular Age* (Cambridge, MA: Harvard University Press, 2007), 473–95, 505–22.

Sadly, a large swath of Western society cannot aim at either achievement or fulfillment. Lacking skills that are in demand, they earn meager wages and hope merely to escape poverty. Many hold several part-time jobs because they cannot find full-time work. Even college graduates find themselves cobbling together a cluster of gigs, hoping that one will eventually lead to a career.

Appraising the Contemporary Scene

Believers will find the contemporary emphasis on individual fulfillment and expression appealing for several reasons. First, because it is the prevailing mind-set, it sounds normal. Second, it seems like an alternative to materialism. Third, it faintly resembles certain biblical ideas. The quest for happiness sounds like the gift of blessedness. The desire to follow one's passions sounds like the idea that everyone should find their gifts—although I wonder if the church's fascination with spiritual gifts is prompted more by cultural trends or Bible study.

The church finds these secular ideas attractive for a reason: it *is* good to realize our potential and find fulfillment at work. The Bible occasionally links work to joy and satisfaction (Deut. 16:15; Prov. 12:14; Eccl. 2:1–26; 8:15; Heb. 13:17). Jesus found satisfaction in accomplishing the work of redemption (Isa. 53:11; John 4:34). But Scripture normally sees work as a place for faithful labor, not a place where we get to choose what we want to do (Num. 12:7; Ezek. 48:11; Matt. 25:21; 1 Cor. 4:17; 7:17–24; 1 Tim. 1:12).

At best, many individualists have a selfless or altruistic streak: they want to earn a living *and* serve the community. They hope for fulfilling labor, but suspect that satisfaction comes when they give to others. Therefore, an individualist may choose to teach in the inner city for less pay and with fewer resources. She may volunteer to work with refugees or prisoners. Happily, there is also enough respect for law and duty in the West to rein in the worst impulses of individualism. We still admire people— parents, firefighters, soldiers—who do their duty whether it is pleasant or not.

That said, we need to do more than endorse the positive threads in contemporary thought. The notion that individual self-expression and self-development are the supreme goals of mankind is novel, in historical terms, and it has harmed both individuals and communities. We need a positive program to reclaim work, which is the goal of the next chapters. Lord willing, we will discover how to find our calling, work faithfully, endure in difficult places, and effect reforms that promote love and justice.

Discussion Questions

1. What is wrong with the Greek concept of work? The medieval concept? Luther's concept?
2. Has your view of work been more like that of the Greeks, the medieval theologians, or the Reformers? What happens when we fail to see our work properly?
3. Do you agree that no job is entirely secular? How does that conviction affect your work? Do you serve God's honor and kingdom while you labor?
4. Why is it important to step back and question the order or structure of work at times?
5. How does Adam Smith explain the way people are alienated from their work? Is his theory still relevant? Given that Marxism is a failed dream, what is the appeal of Marx's view of labor?
6. Is there a place for self-development and self-actualization in a biblical view of work? If so, is it a major theme or a minor theme? How important is it for you?

PART 2

FAITHFULNESS

5

CALLING AND WORK

The Experience of Calling

In 2001, two planes smashed into the World Trade Center. As thousands of office workers dashed *down* the stairs to safety, hundreds of firefighters and rescue workers raced *up* them toward danger, to rescue trapped workers. They knew they might lose their lives, and many did. The nation called the rescue workers heroes, but the firefighters replied, "We're not heroes, we just did our jobs."[1]

The words "I'm no hero, I just did my job" come easily to the lips of people who know their calling and fulfill it. Designers, surgeons, and parents of twins sound the same note. Ordinary people shout their praise and they reply, "Just doing my job." Christians might add, "Yes, it's your job *and* God's calling."

The *experience* of calling is gratifying, and we can recognize a calling in clear cases, but the *concept* has been long fraught with confusion and debate. Classic Roman Catholic theology spoke of callings to the priesthood but not of callings to "secular" work. The Reformers challenged that view. Luther insisted that the milkmaid with her cows, the farmer in his fields, and the magistrate dispensing justice were as pleasing to God, and as important to man, as any priest or monk. Today, however, certain

---

1. By contrast, in 2018, a sheriff's deputy in Parkland, Florida, took cover instead of attempting to stop a shooter who killed seventeen high school students. We might conclude that he had a job, but not a calling.

85

theologians question Luther's notion of calling. They notice that it could lead to passivity, even oppression, if people view their jobs as God's appointed place for them and thus think they must remain in that job.[2] Others notice that the Bible almost always uses the term *calling* to mean God's call to everyone to believe in Jesus. So they wonder if *calling* is the right term for the labor of farmers, magistrates, or those in any other career. Indeed, they ask if Protestants have fused secular notions of fulfillment with biblical notions of calling.

Concepts of Calling

As we saw in the last chapter, Abraham Maslow asserts that once humans meet their needs for food, clothing, shelter, safety, security, and love or acceptance, they pursue higher goals—achievement and self-actualization.[3] Today, most young adults hope that their work will help them find fulfillment and significance, especially if they work hard, consult the right experts, improve themselves, and stay mobile.[4]

Meanwhile many churches still harbor medieval hierarchical notions of calling. Somehow, disciples feel that "business" is second-class spiritually, a notch below "full-time Christian service." Sadly, even pastors can feel that they are second-rate. A seminary professor, who reads and lectures, seems inferior to a pastor, who deals with the gritty problems of ordinary people. But if a missional church starts to rank clergy, pastors may rank below missionaries, who leave the comforts of home and minister in another language! But there are even ranks among missionaries. Those who serve in Africa outdo missionaries serving in comfortable Europe. Among missionaries, evangelists enjoy more esteem than support staff. And *city* evangelists bow to *frontier*

---

2. See discussion of Luther in chapter 3.

3. Abraham Maslow, "A Theory of Human Motivation," *Psychological Review* 50, 4 (1943).

4. Douglas Schuurman, *Vocation: Discerning Our Callings in Life* (Grand Rapids: Eerdmans, 2004), 117–21.

evangelists, who reach people by traversing crocodile-infested waters. Yet no one can surpass pioneer *translators*, who labor without a church. At the pinnacle of Christian workers stands the Bible translator who lives alone in the jungle, without electricity, in a snake-infested tree hut. So it goes.

The interest in ranking work pervades secular society too. In a recent presidential campaign, a reporter found that a leading candidate donated only $600 to charity the previous year, though his annual income approached a million dollars. When questioned about his miserly ways, he replied, "I have given my life to public service." If political work equals public service, the politician may have a point. But when he said he gave meagerly because he served publicly, he implied that a politician need not give *money* because he has already given his *life*.

But we should question our politician. When he claims, "I have given my life to public service," does he imply that bakers, physicians, and garbage collectors have not? If all bakers, truckers, farmers, physicians, garbage collectors, and politicians disappeared on the same day, whom would we miss first?

Perhaps that question is unfair. Whatever occupation we might miss first, we would miss the services of every legitimate and productive vocation in time. Society needs politicians with hearts for justice and the public good, but do pastors, politicians, or physicians serve in a uniquely noble way? That question deserves a careful answer. First, no honest calling is morally superior to any other. Cashiers and corporate leaders, cabinetmakers and icemakers, all have a capacity to serve God and neighbor. He will ask each of us the same questions on the last day:

- Did you honor me by honing the skills I gave you?
- Did you honor the parents, mentors, and friends who invested in you?
- Did you use your abilities to provide for your family?
- Did you promote the good of your neighbors, mankind, and this world?

• Did my people get answers to their legitimate prayers through you?

These questions do not necessarily preclude evaluating various lines of work. The five questions assume that valid work serves society. Sadly, some work that is legal is useless or destructive. Strip clubs are an obvious example. And passing out fliers for going-out-of-business sales seems pointless. What about selling cotton candy, which offers nothing but empty calories? The sugar surge is hard on children and on parents who battle with their children who long for towers of rainbow-colored sweets. But surely some will object that children should be free to enjoy cotton candy. Besides, a reader may ask, who appointed *you* the sugar police? Truly, one person's trash is another's treasure. That said, if workers decide they are producing nothing useful to society, they are wise to seek new jobs. Unfortunately, people can wake up and find themselves in frivolous jobs, marketing trinkets. They want something better, but how can they find it?

Questions about Calling

When my oldest daughter was seven, I spoke at a secluded retreat center ringed by mountains that were sprinkled with streams, plants, and small animals. We cut her loose one day, and she returned with a box of moss, crickets, and newts. Presenting her discoveries, she exulted, "I *love* this. I was *made* for this."

To do what one loves is everyone's goal. Musicians love to perform their favorite music, bakers delight to make delicious pastries, and engineers yearn to solve challenging problems. But how do we find a job we love? Is there a perfect job waiting for us, a job God designed us to do? And if we do find a job that makes us exult, "I was made for this," how can we keep the sensation from slipping away? While it's thrilling to make an audience laugh, stand-up comedians can get tired of their own jokes, just as musicians can grow weary of performing their hits, not to mention the grinding travel they endure. Beyond that, every job has its tedium. Jerry Seinfeld noted that he would spend an hour to shorten a joke by one word; similarly, most musicians labor through take after take when cutting an album.[5] And beyond that, every calling has moments of "taking out the garbage." At worst, work is futile—like trying to raise beef cattle on land suited for bison or trying to grow wheat in drought-ridden plains.[6]

So how do we find and recognize God's call? What if we feel miscast and want a different job, but prospects look dim? What if a person longs to marry and have children, but hopes dwindle? When work is difficult, how can we tell when to persevere and when to move on? What if we sense a readiness for greater responsibilities, but no one offers them? What if a headhunter recruits us to a new position? Is it true that we should feel peaceful and fulfilled if we find the right place? Let's start with the foundation: the biblical teaching on calling.

God Calls His People First to Faith and Union with Christ

When Western Christians speak of their calling, they probably mean their work, but when Scripture speaks of God's call, it normally describes God's call to faith. Theologians label this the "general call" because it goes to everyone. Paul speaks of a call to faith, holiness, and conformity to Christ. Paul tells the Romans they are "*called* to belong to Jesus Christ." Indeed, "all those in Rome" are "loved by God and *called* to be saints" (Rom. 1:6–7). Further, those who love God are "*called* according to his purpose . . . to be conformed to the image of his Son" (8:28–29). Similarly, Paul tells the Corinthians, God "*called* you into fellowship with his Son, Jesus Christ" (1 Cor. 1:9). The call goes both

---

5. A microphone once picked up John Lennon shouting, "I've got blisters on my fingers!"

6. Dan O'Brien, *Buffalo for the Broken Heart* (New York: Random House, 2002); Jonathan Raban, *Bad Land* (New York: Vintage Departures, 1997); Tim Keller, *Every Good Endeavor* (New York: Penguin, 2012), 91–107.

ways when we heed God's voice. The church is *"called* to be his holy people, together with all . . . who *call* on the name of our Lord" (1:2). Paul also commands, *"Take hold* of the eternal life to which you were *called* when you made your good confession" (1 Tim. 6:12). By this call, God graciously brings us to himself (Phil. 3:14). Believers must then confirm their call by holding fast to their convictions (Heb. 3:14; 2 Peter 1:10). But as we'll see, Paul uses *calling* in a different sense in 1 Corinthians 7.

God Calls His People to Places and Roles

According to Scripture, God calls believers to places and roles. This concept is difficult to appreciate if we suffer dissatisfaction at work or dislike our geographical location. It makes us wonder when it will be time to change jobs or relocate. At worst, single adults long to be married, and married adults long to be single. At worst, the college president yearns for the classroom, and a cluster of professors ache to become president. Paul addresses this sense of mislocation when the Corinthian church asks him questions about marriage and slavery. It will be worthwhile to trace his line of thought.

Paul begins with marriage.[7] As a rule, the Corinthians grew up as pagans and therefore married pagans. When Paul preached Christ, many believed. Naturally, converts hoped their spouses would also believe, but when they did not, some wondered if they should divorce an unbelieving spouse.

Paul tells the Corinthians to stay married and fulfill their duties, since marriage is permanent. But they should take comfort because God set apart a believer's family. They should live together in purity and peace (1 Cor. 7:3–5, 10–15). This doesn't mean divorce is always wrong. Certain situations are beyond reconciliation.[8] Paul mentions desertion: no one could force a

---

7. For space, I set aside the question of single people who consider marriage (1 Cor. 7:8–9, 25–38).

8. Again, space forbids that we explore the situations where infidelity or violence might lead to separation or divorce.

spouse to stay in a marriage. If a husband left his wife for distant parts, it was impossible to track him. A believer must not desert a marriage, "But if the unbelieving partner separates, let it be so" (v. 15)—that is, if the unbeliever leaves, the believer must let him or her leave.[9] The principle is simple: *stay* in the marriage *unless* the unbeliever resolves to leave. In that case, "let them go" (NLT) or "agree to it" (CEV).

Paul gives a reason that applies to marriage and to other difficult situations: "How do you know, wife, whether you will save your husband? Or, how do you know, husband, whether you will save your wife?" (7:16). This cuts two ways. It forbids despair: one never knows if an uninterested spouse may yet convert. And it forbids unbound optimism: "If I only pray enough, love him enough, he will convert." Paul asks, "How can you know that?" Paul's question allows a believing spouse to let the unbeliever go. The Lord saves; humans do not. The section concludes: "Only let each person lead the life that the Lord has assigned to him, and to which God has called him" (v. 17). This principle is so essential that Paul restates it in 7:20 and 7:24 and applies it to marriage (vv. 12–13), ethnicity (vv. 18–19), and slavery (vv. 21–23).

The theme "stay, unless, because" pervades 1 Corinthians 7. Paul repeatedly tells disciples in difficult circumstances, "Stay where you are, unless there is strong reason to change." He keeps presenting the "stay, unless, because" principle and keeps adding reasons. Earlier he said, "*Stay* single, *unless* your desires are unmanageable, *because* it is better to marry than to burn" (vv. 8–9). Here he instructs people to *stay* married, *unless* an unbelieving spouse resolves to leave, *because* no one knows if a pagan spouse will believe or not (vv. 12–16).

Next, Paul addresses slavery. Each Corinthian "should remain in the condition in which he was called" (v. 20). If someone is a slave, "Don't be concerned about it." That is, *stay*, "*unless* you can gain your freedom." In that case, "do so" (v. 21 NIV). The

---

9. The Greek verb has the form of a command, not a wish.

reasoning, the *because*, follows. When we belong to Christ, other questions of status become secondary. Specifically, slaves have freedom in the Lord, and the free are the Lord's slaves (v. 22). A Christian should never voluntarily become a slave (v. 23), yet even an enslaved person is free to serve Christ.[10] Therefore, in general, believers "should remain in [their] situation" (v. 24 NIV). Paul's teaching applies to every life circumstance, and the repetition reinforces the point (7:17, 20, 24). There is no universal right to improve one's lot by fleeing hard situations. A difficult marriage, job, family, or city is also God's assignment. A change of circumstances may not solve a problem. We should not desert God's assignment. We should seek contentment there (Phil. 4:10–12).

The call to Christ comes to people in sundry social settings. That call reduces the power of our circumstances, so that we aren't constrained to change our location or position. We can stay where we were when Christ called us.

Paul insists that we respect our God-given station, but he never quite labels our job or our life setting a *calling*. Gordon Fee asserts, "At most 'calling' refers to the circumstances in which the calling [to Christ] took place."[11] John Frame counters that 1 Corinthians says God providentially sends a "walk of life" in marriage, singleness, farming, or carpentry, so that "it's not wrong to find reference to vocation in one's walk."[12] Paul does state that Christians have a "situation the Lord has assigned" (1 Cor. 7:17). Although the Bible never precisely identifies work as a *calling*, it is a reasonable way to label God's assignment to a task.[13]

That Paul never labels slavery a *calling* makes sense, since

---

10. The term *enslaved person* may be superior to the term *slave* because it reminds us that we speak of a person to whom something dreadful has happened.

11. Gordon Fee, *The First Epistle to the Corinthians* (Grand Rapids: Eerdmans, 1987), 309.

12. John Frame, *Systematic Theology: An Introduction to Christian Belief* (Phillipsburg, NJ: P&R Publishing, 2013), 941–42.

13. This use of *calling* resembles the word *Trinity*. Neither appears in the Bible, but both provide useful nomenclature.

slavery is so corrosive. Slavery was a social status and a condition for work, but not a calling. Three times Paul commands his people to stay where they are and fulfill their duties (1 Cor. 7:17, 20, 24). If they have doubts about their ethnic heritage or family history, they should not regard these things as accidents, but as the result of God's sovereign direction (vv. 18–19). So although enslavement is no calling, Paul tells slaves that they have an assignment. They serve Christ there, and "they should not be concerned about it"—that is, their enslaved condition (v. 21). This is astonishing, since a slave had scant legal rights and no control of his or her body. Aristotle called a slave "a living possession," a "talking tool," and "property with a soul."[14] Slaves were liable to beatings, and masters could use them as they willed. How could Paul tell slaves, "Don't let that bother you" (v. 21 CEV)?[15]

Paul doesn't *endorse* slavery; he *transforms* it by teaching that *everyone belongs to someone*. So Paul is radical but not revolutionary. He never calls for a slave revolt, but he attacks slavery's roots by calling himself, Moses, and David slaves of God (Rom. 1:1; 2 Cor. 4:5; Rev. 15:3; cf. Pss. 78:70; 89:3). He even teaches that Jesus took the form of a slave (Acts 3:13; Phil. 2:7).[16]

Everyone lives in some form of bondage. Everyone lives under authority. The secretary belongs to the boss, the boss belongs to the CEO, and the CEO belongs to the stockholders and the board. At college, a student belongs to the professor, the professor belongs to the dean, the dean to the provost, and the provost to the president. A state university president answer to state boards, which answer to the governor, who answers to the citizens. In this way, the presidents and professors belong to the students, if they vote. Everyone serves someone, and many of

---

14. Aristotle, *Politics*, trans. Benjamin Jowett, in *The Basic Works of Aristotle*, ed. Richard McKeon (New York: Random House, 1941), 1131–35 (Book 1, chaps. 4–6).

15. The Greek reads μή σοι μελέτω. A literal rendering might be, "Let it not be a concern to you."

16. See chapter 9.

us serve multitudes.[17] In that sense, no one is free and everyone should serve wherever they are.

Paul is no fatalist. He tells slaves, "If you can gain your freedom, do so" (1 Cor. 7:21). Again, the principle is *stay, unless*. In that culture, enslaved workers could obtain their freedom by using their earnings, since skilled slaves earned the same wages as free people. So it was best to gain freedom, but it was not essential, since slaves could still serve God (v. 22).

To Work in Our God-Given Place May Feel Right— Or Wrong

Let's apply this principle to the people who think work should be more than a place of employment. They think they should find fulfillment, discover their gifts, and flourish at work. Douglas Schuurman remarks that his college students naively view work as "a realm for self-fulfillment" and "optimal self-actualization." Through hard work, consultation with mentors, and the wise use of opportunities, they expect they will find a fulfilling career.[18] But, Schuurman adds, this myth applies (at best) to those who have native intelligence, a network of supportive adults, a strong work ethic, and access to an elite education, by world standards. Those in the lower socioeconomic classes rarely have such opportunities. "Self-actualization" is a chimera for the vast majority of human beings, and even upper-class adults exaggerate their options. In short, everyone needs to hear Paul.

That said, I affirm that we can take pleasure in our work. Romans 12:6–8 instructs believers to exercise their gifts freely and cheerfully, as we serve others. We should enjoy using our gifts. As noted earlier, professors sometimes say, "I teach for free; they pay me to grade papers." I agree. I also speak at conferences for free; they pay me to provide lecture outlines, endure airplanes,

---

17. Survivalists or subsistence farmers may claim to be free from authority. That can be disputed, but the person who wants to answer to no one is probably a slave to the concept of independence.

18. Schuurman, *Vocation*, 117–21.

and sleep in strange beds. That said, even if our best work is joyful, work is rarely the best place to find ourselves.

First Corinthians 7 teaches that work and relationships are not "domains freely chosen" as much as places the Lord assigns. Scholars call this *ascriptivism*—that is, a person's major social relations are not primarily matters of "individual choice, but are assigned based largely on class, family history, and gender. One does not so much choose one's callings as discover oneself" within them. In this view, to find our vocation is not to choose the right spouse, work, friends, or residence; it is to see our web of relationships "as divinely assigned places to serve God and neighbor."[19]

This is an aspect of Paul's teaching that Lutherans and certain Catholics are apt to endorse, due to their tendency to accept existing social structures. Calvinists, with a high view of God's sovereignty, agree that Paul wants people to find themselves where they are. But Calvinists add that *both* individual members of society *and* the "structures of our social world are fallen." Therefore, we must *both* accept our position *and* strive to reform it if we can.[20] So we *stay* wherever we work, *unless* we can move to a better position in our social structure *or* improve the social structure itself, *because* God's people are responsible for themselves and for the wider world.

Paul declares, "You were bought at a price" (1 Cor. 7:23 NIV). Therefore, freeborn people are "Christ's slaves," and slaves who belong to Christ are free. That means no one needs to flee from the bonds of illness, poverty, dull jobs, or flawed families. *Everything* feels like bondage at times, even the best job and family. Yet nothing truly enslaves God's children.

Christians often miss this. A common Christian message goes like this: When you seek God's call, look for a match between the *internal call* (what you *want* to do) and the *external*

---

19. Ibid., 117; Nicholas Wolterstorff, *Until Justice and Peace Embrace* (Grand Rapids: Eerdmans, 1983), 17, 36.
20. Wolterstorff, *Until Justice and Peace Embrace*, 16, 22–23.

call (what an employer is willing to hire you to do). When both come together, you have a call; otherwise you have an aspiration. The standard secular message, which Christians often embrace, says, "Follow your passion." If that fails, gain strategic, well-paid skills.

Given Western society's current emphasis on self-development, we need to help restrain subjective impulses. This is vital, because many people feel a call that no one else detects—to be a musician, perhaps, or to lead a business. But the "follow-your-passion" model is egocentric. It also gives the *initiative* to each person's self-appraisal. The follow-your-passion approach then lets public opinion control our self-evaluation. Therefore, if a man declares, "I want to become an actor," but never lands a part, his counselors will suggest a support position, away from the camera, if he wants to stay in entertainment. Thus, our aspirations do not entitle us to the position we desire. To announce "I want to be an architect" does not make one an architect or even a student of architecture.

To summarize, first, the follow-your-passion approach to calling dominates the Western imagination. Second, the system has clear ways to control people who think their passion must lead to a job. Third, even if we know how to temper the "find-your-passion" enthusiasts, the mind-set still has a problem: it places human aspirations at the center, it gives human correction a secondary role, and it pushes God to the side.

John Frame suggests a God-centered approach. Incorporating the valid insights of the standard Christian message, he argues that a call comes in four ways:

1. God *gives gifts* to humanity and to his people.
2. The Spirit enables people to *discern their gifts* (fallibly) through self-examination and the confirmation of mentors, friends, and colaborers.
3. God *provides opportunities to develop* and exercise those gifts.

4. God grants *wisdom to use gifts* to glorify him and love our neighbor.[21]

By restoring God's role, Frame corrects the tendency to see calling in subjective terms. There is more to calling than one party's desires meeting another party's personnel needs. Still, no one should deny that aspirations or passion have a role. Solomon observes that if a man can "rejoice in his toil," it "is the gift of God" (Eccl. 5:19). And Paul teaches that people should enjoy using their spiritual gifts. Leaders should lead "with zeal," and the merciful should act "with cheerfulness" (Rom. 12:8).

How to Find a Calling

Ideally, a calling begins with an innate or developed ability or skill, coupled with an interest, even a passion, that wells up from the core of one's being. We have a talent when we pick up complex skills quickly. We may have a call if we delight in that talent. For example, a student understands math at once and notices that he can explain it to his classmates more effectively than the teacher does. Perhaps he will be a teacher. Or another young person takes machines apart, grasps their mechanisms immediately, and then reassembles them with ease. Thinking biblically, we call that a gift. When we add mentors and opportunities, a calling may develop.

Mentors are essential. What should these young people do with their abilities in math and mechanics? Mentors watch, appraise, give opportunities, and review the results. They start their mentees with easy duties and assess their performance. Soon an errand includes a wrinkle; the mentor may elect *not* to explain it, to see what happens. The next commission contains a real challenge and a full review afterward. The thoughtful mentor has scant relation to an employer. If a desperate person

---

21. John Frame, *The Doctrine of the Christian Life* (Phillipsburg, NJ: P&R Publishing, 2008), 312–13.

asks us to do a job, it reveals nothing about our gifts. But suppose a superb singer invites an aspiring pianist to practice with his band and she agrees to come. After the practice session, the leader's response is crucial. Does he say, "Thanks for coming" and never call again? Or does he invite her back? If he does, she is seeing the fruit of her labor and should look for more. Perhaps the invitation followed years of preparation. The first sign was the girl's ability to learn songs quickly and sing them sweetly. Her grandmother invited her to play the piano. When they graduated to duets, the girl marveled at the sensation. Practice sessions lengthened and skills grew. The following illustration depicts the way skills emerge and callings arrive.

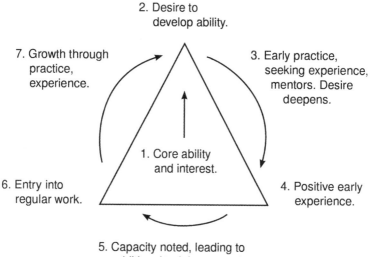

Fig. 5.1. Finding a Calling

If it were possible, this graph would spiral along a time line, to signify the way gifts express themselves as we gain training and experience. Positive experiences foster enthusiasm to learn and grow more. The gifted receive more demanding tasks. One skill leads us to develop similar skills, and our competencies multiply. Eventually we can become experts and then leaders as one opportunity leads to another. Let's imagine the ensuing years for our pianist. After the piano, she picked up the guitar and then the clarinet. Soon she joined a band that needed multi-instrumentalists. After piano, guitar, and clarinet, she learned mandolin, saxophone, and the harmonica. Each instrument seemed easier than the last. She improvised, harmonized, and eventually began to transcribe the best results. Later, organizational abilities emerged, and she formed her own band and negotiated a recording contract.

Where does it all start? Young adults ask themselves questions: *Do I have a desire and ability that lets me meet a need? Remedy a deficit? In a setting that leads to employment?*[22] If there is a glut of pianists, the strategic musician will learn additional instruments. The next questions focus on location: *Which people will I serve? Where will I serve?* Will a young musician hope to teach in elementary school? In high school? In the city, town, or country? Even if a jazz band plays across the globe, it has a fan base and a geographical home. That home base includes people who depend on the band in some way.

Because gifts and passions originate within a person, they have a self-focus, but they should not be self-*ish*. The questions "What can I do well?" and "What do I want to do?" properly lead to "What problems can I solve?" Eventually one should ask, "What burden will I bear?" Every lasting call brings glory and suffering, fulfillment and pain. Our ability to meet needs, whether physical, financial, legal, emotional, or educational, will bring both satisfaction and sorrow.

In the beginning, it is natural to dream of glory, but most callings demand virtues, such as collaboration, and not just skills. On a well-formed team, every member counts. Jason Lezak won

---

22. Dan Allender, *To Be Told* (Colorado Springs, CO: Waterbrook Press, 2005), 113–17.

eight Olympic swimming medals, including four gold, but only one, a bronze, as an individual. He was a relay specialist who swam best with others. Lezak anchored the 4 x 100-meter freestyle relay that helped Michael Phelps win an unprecedented eight gold medals in the 2008 Olympics. The French team, which was favored to win, gave a 0.6-second lead to Alain Bernard, the world's best freestyle swimmer at the time, for the final leg. If Lezak failed to catch Bernard, Phelps would also fail in his quest for eight gold. When Lezak entered the pool, no one thought he had a chance of catching Bernard. Indeed, Bernard's half-body lead *grew* over the first fifty meters. But Lezak kept working. "You're at the Olympics," he told himself. "You can't give up." (Apparently, athletes think about quitting *during their greatest races*.) Lezak started gaining with thirty meters to go. Bernard began to press and lost momentum. With ten meters to go, Lezak was almost even. People screamed, "He's catching up," as Lezak raced for his teammates.

Lezak and Bernard seemed to touch the wall simultaneously . . . then the scoreboard flashed Lezak's triumph. The man who never won a big race as an individual secured his team's gold with the fastest 100-meter swim *of all time*. His team crushed the world record by four seconds, winning on the strength of a relay specialist. Michael Phelps became a household name, but he needed Lezak, the relay specialist. I tell this story because the world has more relay specialists than independent stars. Support roles are essential callings too.

Frederick Buechner says, "The place God calls you to is the place where your deep gladness and the world's deep hunger meet."[23] If Buechner is right, then our call and work are provisional, for the world's hungers shift. We have core abilities and interests that remain through life, but as we grow, our interests and capacities change. As we adjust, our call may change too,

23. Frederick Buechner, *Wishful Thinking: A Theological ABC* (New York: Harper & Row, 1973), 95.

especially as we consider the best way to use our skills to restore this broken world.

Strive to Live Wisely within God's Callings

Gene Veith also expands the way we think of work and other roles. Veith identifies several calls. Beyond work, believers are called to discipleship, family, society, and the church. A retired woman may not work for pay, but she still has callings as mother, grandmother, citizen, disciple, sister, and friend.[24] A college student has several callings too. He is a student, a roommate, a guard on an intramural basketball team, and a barista at a coffee shop. Given that everyone has several callings, changes are inevitable. But, Veith continues, we shouldn't focus on that, as if the right calling is around the corner. Society ascribes various weights to these activities, but all have moral value, because God issues them.[25]

So let's question the question "What do you want to be when you grow up?" Children may reply that they want to be a fighter pilot or a ballerina, but not many have the requisite skills for either. "What do you want to do?" is a sensible question, but there are others: Who are you? What are your talents? Of the things you can do, which match your personality, your soul?

Yet we must limit this line of thought, too, since Western culture unduly exalts *choosing*. God *appoints* places for his people. The norm is to stay there, *unless* God grants us freedom to change, whether by moving to another job or by reshaping our workplace. In one sense, our callings are beyond our control, for they come from external sources. From outside, God gives gifts and opportunities. Disasters and injuries may derail our plans and yet fulfill his purposes, for the difficulty may drive us into an unforeseen opportunity. I know a man who was fired from a broadcasting enterprise for absurd reasons. Without delay,

---

24. Gene Edward Veith Jr., *God at Work: Your Christian Vocation in All of Life* (Wheaton, IL: Crossway, 2002), 47–49.

25. Ibid., 49–50.

he started a niche network; its success exceeded expectations. From God's perspective, even the darkest developments are part of his plan.[26] So then, we don't simply choose our vocation. We look for appealing work and hope it is a calling, but we also find our calling by working where we are. Whether we move or not, whether we can reform our workplace or not, we should think, "This is my work, the place the Lord assigned."[27]

This is teaching that our restless age needs. When in distress, we should not think first of a new job, city, marriage, or social circle. The great factors for happiness in any place are the Lord's direction and our character, and God is everywhere and we take ourselves wherever we go. Let us therefore persevere, remaining faithful where we are and trusting the Lord who sovereignly bestowed our gifts and who lets us use them in the way he judges best.

Discussion Questions

1. How do you answer the questions in this chapter: Do you have desires and abilities that let you meet needs? Remedy deficits? Can you do so in a setting that leads to employment? What people will you serve? Where can you serve?

2. Do you have a lingering suspicion that "full-time Christian service" is superior to other callings? How would you answer your own doubts about the value of "secular" callings?

3. Do you believe your current *job* is your *calling*? Why or why not?

4. What do people ask you to do? What do you love to do? Where do you bear most fruit? Do people agree with your self-assessment? Why or why not?

26. Ibid., 55.
27. Ibid., 57–59.

6

FAITHFULNESS AT WORK

The Challenge of Faithfulness

An aspiring writer recently asked an advice columnist for counsel and lamented, "I've always wanted to write, and I have—but all the wonderful, inspiring, labor-of-love type things I want to do I can't, because I seemingly can't keep myself from wasting hours of my day on Instagram."[1] Instagram may be long dead by the time anyone reads this text, but that is precisely the point: our distractions rarely *last*.

Managing distractions is one of many challenges that relate to faithfulness at work. Subjectively, we have problems with Instagram, gossip, games, frivolous discussions of sports and movies, and the temptation to track the news all day long.[2] Much of our work seems to produce little of lasting value. Many of us wonder if our job will (or should) exist in seven years.

Once, when Jesus distinguished the externally good works of the Pharisees from the path of genuine discipleship, he declared, "The weightier matters of the law [are] justice and mercy and

---

1. Heather Havrilesky, "I Want to Be a Writer, But I Can't Stop Wasting My Time on Instagram!," Ask Polly, *The Cut*, November 15, 2017, https://www.thecut.com/2017/11/ask-polly-i-cant-stop-wasting-my-life-on-instagram.html. While you're wasting time on this footnote, I'll confess my primary time waster: looking up statistics and quotations on the Internet.

2. I do not mention darker problems, like arriving at work hung over or exhausted because you've mismanaged your time.

faithfulness" (Matt. 23:23). That leads us to ask, "How can I be faithful to God's purposes for work, even if I find myself in a job I dislike at a company whose products I might not use?" What is the path or narrative of a faithful work life? Romantics contend that we should follow our dreams and passions, but professional career advisors call that the highway to poverty. They counsel young adults to gain marketable skills, to set reasonable career goals (whether related to income, power, or freedom), and to strive for them daily. Maybe later, they add, one can chase a dream or try to change the world.

Consider four young believers who pursue faithfulness at work. They grasp the first principles of work. They believe work is good. They want to love their neighbors and care for creation, according to their abilities. They want to work heartily, for the Lord, but they find it difficult because they question their actual jobs.[3]

Abby landed a position with a large retail company when she finished college, but corporate life frustrated her. She squeezed into a tiny, windowless office, crunching numbers and setting price points to maximize sales and profits for a line of clothing that seemed frumpy to her.

Abby's work seemed meaningless until her supervisor told her to visit one of her company's stores and observe the clothes for which she managed pricing. She overheard two women discuss the sweaters she marketed—and scorned. They examined one sweater carefully. One concluded, "You can see that these are well-made. They'll last." Her friend added, "This one is perfect for our Christmas party. I'd buy three if I could afford them."

These comments triggered an epiphany for Abby: "It hit me; these *are* quality sweaters at a fair price. It isn't my job to get middle-aged women to buy what *I* would like. Who am I to judge what styles should please them? My work makes life a little better

---

3. All four are based on real people and real conversations. Two are composites.

for these women if I provide sweaters *they* like." She was faithful to God and her commercial neighbors by joining the production chain that clothes humanity.

Kyle, a financial planner, confronted a tougher challenge. He recently gained his first major client, a childless couple with substantial wealth. But he soon learned that the wife wanted to donate most of their estate to a leading provider of abortion services. This stunned Kyle, a life-affirming disciple. He asked, "How can I build the wealth of a client who plans to give it to a cause I consider immoral?" His company's policies will not let him say, "I can't help you with *that.*" Is he obligated to sever his relationship with the client? But recusing himself wouldn't help, since the money would still go to abortion services.

Kyle decided to research his company's policies and found that he was free to explore a client's values. He could ask, "Why do you want to give to support abortion services?" When he asked, he found that the woman wanted to help women in distress. Kyle immediately recognized that he and the woman had common ground. He told his client, "I admire your desire to help women in distress. I decided to look into a variety of agencies that can help you accomplish that goal." Kyle then described scholarships for job training programs that focus on poor women, and he mentioned the problem of sex trafficking in their city. The woman eventually decided to diversify her will. Kyle believed he was faithful since he was able to help his client achieve her goals while leading her to reallocate her resources to more ethical causes.

Abby and Kyle both pursued faithfulness as professionals, but others have fewer skills and less status. Lisa works in retail, as a cashier. She likes the work, even though it's repetitive, but she wonders if she should aim higher. She also worries that automation may soon replace a major part of her job. Her friend Ryan drives a bread truck and occasionally delivers portable restrooms. He also worries that machines will replace him. He knows people need bread and that portable commodes are essential for construction projects, parades, and outdoor concerts. But he feels that his work is meaningless and laments, "I never *create* anything, I just deliver things—*calories* and *toilets.*"

Lisa and Ryan both have honest jobs, but their church cannot seem to discuss work in ways that help them. Their pastor affirms that all work matters to God, but his illustrations tend toward clearly *productive* vocations: doctors, teachers, engineers, and farmers. When their pastor mentions service, he names volunteer activities that are "churchy": serving in the nursery, hosting a home Bible study, and visiting people in the hospital. None of these connect with Lisa and Ryan, who are single adults living in small apartments and working at modest jobs.

As believers, Lisa and Ryan want to practice their faith at work. They heard that God calls them to govern the world for him, but, like Abby and Kyle, they struggle with unseen results. They can't detect how their work serves God or neighbors. Perhaps this is no surprise, since certain branches of Christendom devalue ordinary labor. Various pastors still reserve the term *calling* for church work. They may think doctors and teachers have a vocation, but they call most paid labor a *job*, not a calling.

Lisa, Ryan, and their pastor need a broader concept of faithfulness. The narrow definition of fidelity goes like this: faithful Christians work hard, operate with moral integrity, share the faith whenever possible, support their family, and give generously if they prosper. These are good points. Indeed, it *is* good to be productive and to resist the temptations to moral compromise. But there is more to fidelity in the workplace.

Consider Jack, a businessperson who has devised ways to transport everything from lipstick to construction cranes with unprecedented efficiency. He also distributes wheat and corn from grain elevators to trains, then barges, and on to consumers all over the world. Because he sees ways to streamline the process, his firm is profitable. If he spoke to Lisa, Ryan, and Abby, he might say this:

I have an ability to apply technology in ways that other people miss. I've learned to move tons of grain a little faster, with less waste, than anyone else. For years, I thought my work was self-ish, that I was just earning money, proving myself, providing for my family, winning the game. Eventually I realized that I was serving people, lots of people, by getting grain to them reliably and efficiently, so they had a steady supply of food at a better price.

God Values All Honest Labor

Many people have trouble seeing the value of their work. In truth, *work is the chief place where we love our neighbors as ourselves.* At work, we have the greatest skill and training, we spend the most time, and we can bring the greatest resources to bear. Jesus' parable of the sheep and the goats, in Matthew 25, describes the value of ordinary work. It describes the last day, when we all stand before the Lord, who appraises our work, and separates his sheep from the goats. Jesus says:

> Then the King will say to those on his right, "Come, you who are blessed by my Father, inherit the kingdom prepared for you from the foundation of the world. For I was hungry and you gave me food, I was thirsty and you gave me drink, I was a stranger and you welcomed me, I was naked and you clothed me, I was sick and you visited me, I was in prison and you came to me." Then the righteous will answer him, saying, "Lord, when did we see you hungry and feed you, or thirsty and give you drink? And when did we see you a stranger and welcome you, or naked and clothe you? And when did we see you sick or in prison and visit you?" And the King will answer them, "Truly, I say to you, as you did it to one of the least of these my brothers, you did it to me." (Matt. 25:34–40)

The Lord watches and assesses all our work, because it publicly demonstrates our faith. At work, we have the greatest capacity to care for the hungry, the thirsty, and the sick. If, by faith, we consecrate our work to God and love our neighbors, clients, and customers, he will remember it forever. Jesus' words touch the main realms of productive labor:

- If our work has *any* role in bringing food to the hungry, Jesus is pleased.
- If we have *any* place in the chain that brings water to the thirsty, he smiles.
- If our work provides *any* clothing or shelter to people, Jesus rewards us.
- If our work has *any* role in the system that brings health or physical care to the sick, Jesus counts it as service to him.[4]

When Jesus says, "I was in prison and you visited me," he blesses all who help the needy. Jesus' teaching also challenges secular perspectives. As we have said, people tend to look for fulfillment at work. Like most essentially secular ideas that Christians adopt, the quest for fulfillment and self-realization is partially valid. Scripture *does* link work and satisfaction. Moses says, "The LORD your God will bless you in all . . . the work of your hands, and your joy will be complete" (Deut. 16:15 NIV; cf. Prov. 12:14; Eccl. 8:15; Heb. 13:17). Jesus found satisfaction in completing his work (Isa. 53:11; John 4:34).

But the quest for fulfillment is largely egocentric. The pursuit of fulfillment readily pushes aside the needs of neighbors. Scripture speaks most often of faithfulness, not fulfillment, in labor. God commends Moses, noting, "He is faithful in all my house" (Num. 12:7; cf. Ezek. 48:11). Jesus will bless his people on the last day, "Well done, good and faithful servant" (Matt. 25:21, 23). And Paul teaches, "It is required of stewards that they be found faithful" (1 Cor. 4:2; cf. 4:17; 1 Tim. 1:12). So then, everyone

---

4. Lester DeKoster, *Work: The Meaning of Your Life* (Grand Rapids: Christian Library Press, 1982), 22–27.

who works with justice and fidelity in finance, transportation, administration, and management participates in Jesus' blessing. That is why the work of truck drivers and retail workers counts.

Every Contribution Is Significant

I interviewed four people who worked in transportation, two leaders and two drivers, for this book. All four struggle, at times, to see the value of their work. They tend to lament, "I just deliver stuff; I don't *make* anything." The cure is a wider perspective. Suppose they deliver food. Where would consumers be without the trains and trucks that distribute food? Will they *drive themselves* to Kansas to buy a cow, to Idaho for potatoes, to Minnesota for wheat? If we reflect, we realize that everyone in the chain of production contributes to the food supply. Furthermore, in an essential way, no human being actually *grows food*. Suppliers sell seeds, fertilizer, targeted herbicides, and equipment, while farmers till the ground, plant seeds, and harvest the crops, but God sends sun and rain to kiss sleeping seeds awake. Humans can *enhance productivity* in many ways, but God created plant life and providentially orders the conditions that unleash their God-given potential to grow. After the harvest, food processors, packagers, truck drivers, stock boys, and cashiers have their roles. The cashier seems as marginal as the driver. But remember, consumers need to *acquire* their food somehow. Cashiers either take the money or tend machines that transfer money, so the cashier has a vital role. Besides, she is the last person a shopper sees, so she can help an unpleasant shopping trip end well. She fosters customer loyalty by caring for clients. In that way, she loves people at work.

Finite human beings have difficulty appreciating the value or effect of their labor. Consider schoolteachers. The mathematics teacher doesn't know that her former algebra student is now an engineer who designed the efficient bridge she crosses on the way to work. The art teacher doesn't know that his former student sketched a new building he admires daily as he passes it. When I was in graduate school, I felt an urge to write to my fourth-grade teacher, Mrs. Wolf, to thank her for her diligence:

You taught me in fourth grade, and I caused you endless grief. I didn't listen to you because I was always trying to make everyone laugh. You moved me away from my friends after one week. After a month, you put me in a corner and surrounded me with well-behaved girls. You scolded me for failing to reach my potential and punished me with Cs I didn't deserve. You made my naughtiness miserable, and I'm writing to thank you for it. I moved before fifth grade. Since I had no friends, I paid attention. My grades shot up and no one was scolding me for a change. It was so pleasant, I've kept it up ever since.

A month later, I heard from my old school. "Thank you for writing. Your teacher died last month, but I'm sure she would have been glad to read your letter." My heart sank. Mrs. Wolf never knew that her discipline of that mischievous boy made a difference. Teachers ask, "Is anyone listening?" Physicians wonder, "Will my patients take their medicine? Change their destructive habits?" Many ask, "If I disappear, will the machine grind along without me? Does my work make a difference?"

Imagine a woman who tends the drive-through window at a fast-food restaurant. She thinks, "Do these people know how much salt and fat are in this meal? Would it be better if we closed?" But many of us recall the time we drove along, late at night, praying, "Lord, help me find food for the last stretch of this journey." Then we saw a sign and relaxed. The Lord answered our prayer for food through people who were more important than they knew. Loan officers express similar doubts: "I crunch numbers and move money to generate profits for my bank, but I don't *make* anything." But the decision to make a loan may start a business venture that eventually employs hundreds of workers. The Lord sees the value of our work even when we cannot.

By God's grace, we do more good than we know. As a guest

speaker and interim pastor, I often speak to strangers, throwing ideas into the air, wondering if they have any purchase. One day, a woman waited for me at a church where I preached for months. She began, "I have to tell you—your messages saved my life. I was so depressed that I thought about killing myself every day. But every week I dragged my body to church, and the message I heard about God's love and grace gave me a reason to stay alive—and to come back the next week." It took great courage for that woman to tell her story, and it is unusual but not unique. Because I was still preaching, she could find me. Normally, we can't find the farmers, food processors, and truck drivers who bring us food, but if we could, we should shout, "Thank you for feeding me!"

God gives everyone a role as well as a place of service. We pray, "Give us this day our daily bread," and God calls farmers, truck drivers, and cashiers to collaborate to bring us bread. When Jesus blesses his people on judgment day, he will say, "I was hungry and you gave me food, . . . I was sick and you looked after me." We will ask, "When?"

We tend to think that we feed the hungry when we volunteer in a soup kitchen, but that is shortsighted. We serve most effectively in paid positions (and in the home) because we work so long and skillfully there. So Jesus tells disciples that whatever good we do, we do it to him and for him (Matt. 25:35–40).

At work we have the greatest capability to meet legitimate human needs. If, by faith, we consecrate our work to God and aim to love both our coworkers and our customers, we serve the Lord and he remembers it. When Jesus says, "I was in prison and you came to me," he blesses all acts of compassion. Everyone who consciously serves God, according to his standards, has his approval, whether they work in construction, energy, finance, or transportation.

We need to broaden our horizons here. Consider the phrase, "I was a stranger." Our work welcomes strangers if it keeps people connected so they never become strangers in the first place. So all who "work in communications of any kind" welcome the stranger by helping people "sustain relationships" that create "a sense of shared humanity and identity."[5]

Sadly, a great deal of communication *separates* people through misinformation, rumor, and fearmongering. That is another reason for believers to work faithfully in communication. Every industry is susceptible to abuse, even those that meet basic needs, like the need for food. Farmers give us juicy plums, but grocery stores also sell nutritionless junk food. Much of human work battles sin and its results. That is why the world needs disciples in every honest calling. The goodness of our work calls for hope, while its fallenness demands our perseverance.

The Struggle for Meaning Is Universal

We might imagine that people who perform humble tasks struggle most with disappointment at work, but no one does whatever he wants to do, not even a king. As king of Israel, David had a zeal for worship (2 Sam. 6). Once God gave David rest from his enemies, he resolved to build a temple for the Lord (7:1–2). David told Nathan the prophet, who quickly approved the project. But God rebuked Nathan, reminding him, essentially, that prophets *just might* want to consult him before speaking in his name. The Lord explained that David was "a man of war" who had "shed blood" and therefore could not build the temple (1 Chron. 28:3). The Lord wanted people to find peace with him at the temple. Therefore, Solomon, a man of peace, had to build it (22:8–9).

David's disappointment shows that everyone has dashed hopes and thwarted plans. God called David to fight Israel's enemies in justified defensive campaigns. Still, David had bloody hands and God vetoed his proposal. But David accepted God's decision and embraced a secondary role in the temple's construction, supporting his son in the task (1 Chron. 22:7). He blessed Solomon, assured him of God's presence, donated vast sums of

---

5. Greg Forster, "Work and the Meaning of Life: Key Insights from Lester DeKoster," in *Educational Pathways Project, Foundational Ideas,* Kern Pastor's Network, 5.

gold, silver, and timber to the project, and commanded Israel's leaders to support Solomon too (vv. 11–19). Indeed, David did so much for the temple that it could almost be called "David's temple," but he remained behind the scenes. Everyone tastes disappointment at work, but work remains meaningful if we accept our God-given roles and support others in theirs, even when we are disappointed.

Talented, ambitious people need to contemplate this, for they often aspire to leadership positions that are not open. Perhaps they yearn for prestige and wealth and need to suspend or quash their aspirations. Or perhaps they believe they can do the work better than the current chief. But even if they *can* do better, they should stop striving to become the executive and consider how best to serve in their place and to support their God-given leader.

By working in our place, we become agents of God's providential care. Through our hands, God answers the prayers of his children. We pray for safety in travel, and engineers design reliable vehicles. When we work faithfully, the naked are clothed, the hungry fed, and the ignorant educated. So we love our neighbors as ourselves at work. Not all work is honest, but all honest work has dignity and therefore merits careful attention. That said, one issue remains.

Are All Callings Equal?

There is a paradox in Christian rhetoric about work, which we began to explore in the first chapter. On the one hand, we stress that all work is honorable and has equal value in God's sight. One the other hand, we exhort people to do work that matters, to work *strategically*. And that implies that all work is *not* equal. The reason for this tension is clear. All labor is equal in some ways but unequal in others. All honest work is equal in that we can consecrate it to the Lord, who sees and rewards it all, as Scripture often teaches (Gen. 15:1; Ps. 28:4; Matt. 16:27; Col. 3:24; Rev. 22:12). Every morally good task has dignity, whether the laborer sweeps floors or runs a company.

But human labor varies in manifold ways. It differs in the skills, preparation, and training required. It differs in pay or economic value and in social esteem. It differs in the burdens borne, in the level of responsibility, in the number of people who depend on the worker's success. The chief executive officer has more influence than his janitor, the judge has more authority than the bailiff, the surgeon has more potential to heal than the scalpel scrubber.

Thus, the farmer who shovels manure can please God as completely as the botanist who breeds disease-resistant, high-yield seeds. Indeed, the shoveler may please God more, if his motives and dispositions are purer. The same holds for the scalpel scrubber and the surgeon.

But suppose the finest surgeons also excel at washing scalpels. Will they please the Lord if they give up surgery to devote themselves to scalpels? Probably not. If they muse, "The stress of surgery is intense," or, "By cleansing scalpels, I will become more humble," we might question their motives: Is this a symptom of stress and exhaustion? Does this person have the temperament for surgery? But given their skill and talent, we might reply, "Please seek counseling and a more humane schedule to reduce stress and find humility, but God has entrusted talents to you and lives are at risk. People depend on you for excellence as a surgeon." Great prophets such as Elijah and Jeremiah became so discouraged that they wanted to quit, but the Lord provided for them and expected them to continue (1 Kings 19:1–18; Jer. 20:1–18; 36:1–38:13).

The goal, the ideal, is to serve God with our highest and rarest gifts. If a man has matchless skills in a strategic field and reaches them by arduous training, he should use those skills. A gifted chef rightly aspires to lead a kitchen, no matter how well she washes pots, chops onions, or concocts potato soup. And a surgeon should operate, no matter how well he washes scalpels. Every calling is holy and everyone should seek the right motives to work, but not everyone has the same ability to do strategic work. Because many can wash scalpels and only a few excel at surgery, surgeons most please God when they use their rarified training and experience to heal the sick.

What Is the Right Place for Ambition?

Leadership is grand but arduous. Leaders typically toil longer hours. Transformational leaders endure stress and opposition, as scientists like Copernicus and Galileo discovered. Reformers must offer ample evidence for the changes they propose. They need to gather followers who can disseminate and defend their ideas or programs. In short, we need people who aspire to lead, despite the hardships. These realities deter talented people who could lead but seek a simple life. But Jesus says something that the talented but unambitious need to consider: "From everyone who has been given much, much will be demanded" (Luke 12:48 NIV). If God gives great gifts, he asks great service. Indeed, Paul declares, "I make it my ambition to preach the gospel" where Christ is not known (Rom. 15:20).[6]

Trailblazers and organizational leaders ought to steward their rare gifts. Nations need the best possible governors, and corporations need the most talented and virtuous executives. Therefore, it is sensible for people with high energy and gifts to strive for leadership. If *ten* physicians can perform routine surgeries well but only *one* can improve surgical procedures, then the one should probably see surgical innovation as his calling. The typical surgeon heals one patient at a time, but the innovator has the ability to serve hundreds. So then, if opportunity for wider service never comes, we serve cheerfully in our place. But if we are qualified for a strategic task and it finds us, we should be open to it. If possible, we should ignore questions of salary and status, since strategic tasks may not offer tangible rewards.

Isaiah 32:1–2 describes the way leaders potentially change a

---

6. The Greek term φιλοτιμεῖσθαι is also used positively in 2 Corinthians 5:9 and 1 Thessalonians 4:11.

city: "Behold, a king will reign in righteousness, and princes will rule in justice. Each will be like a hiding place from the wind, a shelter from the storm, like streams of water in a dry place." Ultimately, this king is Jesus, but Isaiah 32 applies to all who rule under him. When princes—secondary leaders—operate as Jesus' vice-regents, people find shelter in life's storms. Leaders *can* bring shelter. Therefore, if you are a prince, prepare to step forward and lead, if summoned, even if the prestige is lower and the hours longer. That is the way of Jesus, the king who dared to serve.

In summary, the shape of faithfulness varies according to our gifts and settings. Cashiers, drivers, investment bankers, teachers, architects, engineers, and politicians should all see work as their place to love God and neighbor and strive to serve there faithfully. Whether our lot seems humble or exalted, let us work with all our heart, for the Lord knows and rewards all faithful labor.

Discussion Questions

1. What is the prime challenge as you strive to be faithful at work, paid or unpaid: Distractions? Devaluation of your job? Longing for a different job?
2. Why is it hard to be faithful when we don't have the job we long for? What can we learn from David's response when God determined that Solomon would build the temple?
3. In what sense are all callings equal? In what sense are they different?
4. Was Kyle faithful when he decided to coach the couple with an interest in abortion services? Was he restraining evil or compromising? Does his strategy help workers in similar positions?
5. Does your work ever seem meaningless? How did this chapter answer your concern? Do you have friends who think their work is meaningless? How would you encourage them?

7

WORK IN DIFFICULT PLACES

Mike was the chief financial officer of a media corporation that produced news content for magazines, radio, and television. One year, however, his corporation acquired a television program that "entertained" its viewers with lurid tales of sex, violence, and betrayal. Next, it bought a small video company that produced pornography. Mike had no contact with these enterprises, but as the chief financial officer (CFO), he could not claim to be *entirely* disengaged. Several of Mike's Christian friends told him he had to resign. As they saw it, Mike always courted danger by working for a public media company. Now the long-expected conflict between his faith and his work had come.[1]

Mike saw the situation differently. Instead of resigning, he took his concern to the next board meeting. He told the directors that the company's recent acquisitions violated both its principles and its charter. Therefore, it was right and necessary for the corporation to divest itself of both properties. The board resisted, arguing that they followed sound business practices by diversifying their holdings.

Mike replied, "You can call it diversification. But owning a pornography producer violates our charter and when the regulatory agencies find out, we'll be in trouble."

---

1. Each story in this chapter describes real people and events with changes in secondary details.

A board member objected, "There is nothing in the transaction that would reveal the nature of their work. How would they find out?"

Mike explained, "They will find out because I plan to tell them."

"You'll do *what*?" the chairman shouted.

Mike calmly replied, "I will tell them, because I am morally and legally bound to do so."

Mike knew he was right about the need to inform regulators, but it was still a high-risk strategy. Fortunately, his corporation soon sold both ventures and returned to its core enterprises.

Mike faced a dramatic variation of a common question for Christians who work in large, complex organizations. What should we do when our company acts in ways that seem morally questionable? Should we resign? Remain and bring salt and light into the company? Pursue a middle course by staying employed while searching for another job? Some stay permanently and risk the loss of their integrity. Might that be necessary if one has dependents and alternatives are few?

Consider Lisa, a software engineer. Her boss selected her to lead a project designed to make her state's lottery more profitable. Lisa liked the project's technical challenges and thought she could create a more efficient, hence more profitable, system. However, she knew that lotteries prey on the poor. Lisa's rank and reputation in her firm will let her decline and choose another project, but what if she had just been hired and had no choice?

Finally, Libby markets an agricultural firm that feeds vast numbers through high-yield, pest-resistant, genetically-modified seeds. Their plants also help the environment, since they need less water and fewer pesticides. But the seeds are expensive, which hurts marginal farmers, and Libby has doubts about the downstream effects of altering plant DNA. She also feels uneasy when pressed to write copy that exaggerates the strengths and hides the weakness of her client's products.

The experiences of Mike, Lisa, and Libby are common. Large,

complex businesses tend to create moral dilemmas and temptations to compromise for morally alert employees. Believers may ask themselves: Do I need to withdraw from diversified enterprises and work solely for companies I fully support? But all organizations, even churches and Christian schools, face moral dilemmas. Faithful farmers treat their animals with dignity, but they also need to stay profitable, and the way to do both can be uncertain. Profitability and stewardship clash in the grocery store too, since lucrative snack food often has harmful levels of sugar, salt, and additives. How does a car mechanic decide when to tell a customer who loves an old car that it's time to scrap it rather than continue to pay for repairs? And how do medical personnel determine when to treat a dying patient and when to withdraw care that prolongs the process of dying?

Drawing on Scripture, this chapter argues that believers *may* remain in compromised or even corrupt organizations, *if* they can mitigate evil there and if they are not *required* to sin. On the other hand, the godly may also stand outside morally compromised structures and denounce them.

Believers don't normally make decisions on the basis of foreseen consequences, partly because it's so hard to foresee future events. Still there is a time to ask, "What would happen if I were asked to . . ." If a believer works for a deceitful manager who asks him to play along, he knows he must refuse. But what if all believers decided that godliness required them to leave complex, partially tainted organizations? What if, to avoid potential problems, disciples left the military, law, government, and entertainment because they could foresee a moral dilemma?

If believers object to corporate and military conduct now, imagine the result if every Christian influence were taken away from them. Indeed, to achieve complete purity, believers would need to break all social contact and become self-contained, self-employed farmers, monks, and artisans. Unfortunately, monks and farmers can become corrupt, too, even in splendid isolation. Fortunately, Scripture sheds light on our issue.

Basic Principles

To make progress on a controversial topic, we first state the foundational principles and treat them as boundaries for discussion and action. Ideally, that will allow us to determine when we can and cannot be flexible. First, believers may never take jobs that *require* sin, either occasionally or permanently—especially ongoing sin. No believer may kill for hire. God-honoring work is honest and lawful. Second, if work provides the essentials of life—food, clothing, and shelter—it is almost certainly constructive. Third, the Bible instructs disciples to engage their culture and shows them doing so in challenging situations. Paul forbade any effort to separate from all evildoers. To do that, he notes, we would "need to go out of the world," which is not an option (1 Cor. 5:9–11). Fourth, biblical narratives show believers working in daunting environments, chiefly by serving pagan rulers, and maintaining integrity there. We begin with two Israelites in Pharaoh's court.

To Work or Not to Work for Pharaoh

The pharaohs of Egypt were autocrats. Whatever we think of power-hungry politicians today, none match the pharaohs, who (theoretically) claimed deity and ownership of the entire land of Egypt. Nonetheless, when one pharaoh dreamed of lean cows eating fat cows, Joseph interpreted the dream for him. The cows represented seven years of abundance followed by seven years of famine. When Joseph urged Pharaoh to save the coming surplus for impending years of poverty, Pharaoh was so impressed that he made Joseph his second in command. Thus, Joseph served a pagan ruler whose political system rested on blasphemous, egomaniacal claims. Still, by working for this pharaoh, Joseph preserved many lives, including lives in his family, God's covenant family. So he demonstrated that the faithful *may* work for anyone.

Nonetheless, four hundred years later Moses *refused* to serve a different pharaoh, although that man was like a stepfather to him. Moses was born to a Jewish mother, but Pharaoh's daughter adopted him into the royal family. Hebrews says that Moses "refused to be known as the son of Pharaoh's daughter. He chose to be mistreated along with the people of God rather than to enjoy the pleasures of sin for a short time" (Heb. 11:24–27 NIV, 1984 version). By faith, he led Israel out of Egypt through a series of conflicts with Pharaoh (Ex. 5–14).

We can see why each man chose his course. Joseph served one pharaoh to save lives. Moses refused to serve another pharaoh, also to save lives. Why did Moses do this? First, Moses had a distinct calling: to lead Israel out of Egypt. Second, recent Pharaohs had resolved to exterminate or at least enslave God's people (Ex. 2–5). The contrasting decisions of Joseph and Moses show that believers may or may not work for evil masters, depending on their circumstances and calling. The following accounts of Elijah and Obadiah make similar points.

To Work or Not to Work for Ahab

Ahab was a leading candidate for the title "Worst King of Israel." After Solomon died, Israel divided and became two nations. The northern kings spurned God's law and temple. Among northern kings, Ahab "did more evil" than anyone, especially by worshiping Baal (1 Kings 16:30–34). When his pagan wife, Jezebel, killed God's prophets, Ahab did nothing to stop her. And he showed contempt for God's law by confiscating whatever he coveted and killing those who stood in his way (21:1–16).

"Surely," we might think, "no believer could work for Ahab." Indeed, God called Elijah to stand outside Ahab's court and declare judgment in the form of drought and famine (17:1). After three years of drought, Elijah returned to confront Ahab. Yet Elijah came first, not to Ahab, but to his palace manager, Obadiah: "Obadiah was a devout believer in the LORD. While Jezebel was killing off the Lord's prophets, Obadiah had taken a hundred prophets and hidden them in two caves, fifty in each, and had supplied them with food and water" (18:3–4 NIV).

We wonder how Obadiah could govern the palace of a king

such as Ahab. Had Obadiah's father been a courtier? Had he come to faith after taking his role? Whatever his path to power, Obadiah believed he could serve God's people in a dark but strategic place. By staying in Ahab's court, Obadiah had opportunity to undermine Ahab's rule, although he took great risks, since Ahab was a violent man (18:9–14). Surely Obadiah's life was forfeit if Ahab had found out that Obadiah had sheltered the very prophets the king wanted to exterminate. But Ahab trusted Obadiah, and as the drought wore on, Ahab dispatched his manager to find water. As Obadiah searched, Elijah met him. Obadiah recognized Elijah, and bowed before him (18:7). Elijah told Obadiah, "Go tell your master, 'Elijah is here'" (18:8 NIV).

Obadiah protested that if he told Ahab of Elijah's presence, the Spirit would whisk away the prophet and Ahab would kill Obadiah for a false report. Yet, he adds, "I your servant have worshiped the LORD since my youth . . . [and] hid a hundred of the Lord's prophets" (18:12–13 NIV). Then Elijah assured Obadiah, "I will surely present myself to Ahab today" (18:15 NIV).

It is easy to hurry past this encounter to reach the climax of the story, when Elijah defeats the prophets of Baal. But let's pause to notice the lesson about work. We see that God can ask his agents to serve him in contrasting ways. Elijah served God by *standing outside the king's court*, while Obadiah served God by *staying within the king's court*. Elijah *denounced* the king's regime from the outside, but *Obadiah kept silent* and organized relief for the prophets from the inside. Elijah *protested* evil while Obadiah *restrained* evil.

Different as they were, Elijah and Obadiah respected the other's role. Obadiah called Elijah "my lord," and Elijah accepted Obadiah as Ahab's manager. Neither criticized the other; neither recruited the other. Each knew what God wanted him to do, and both knew God had *different* work for his brother. When Elijah assured Obadiah that he would be safe, he implied that Obadiah rightly stayed in Ahab's court. Both men were faithful in dealing with Ahab.

The lesson is clear. If Obadiah could serve God while working for Ahab, then believers may work for almost anyone, *if* they can serve God there. We can work in corrupt enterprises, if we resist compromise, restrain evil, and promote justice. Scripture never encourages believers to court danger by seeking employment in a corrupt organization, but when evil finds us, we should resist it (James 4:7; 1 Peter 5:9).

It is permissible to avoid hostility by fleeing (Matt. 10:23), or we may stay where we are, despite the danger. Jesus modeled both tactics. He fled an angry crowd in Nazareth in Luke 4. And three years later, he stood his ground in Jerusalem, although it led to his crucifixion. Depending on his goals, Jesus could act like Elijah or like Obadiah. Like Elijah, Jesus pronounced judgment on a corrupt generation. Like Obadiah, Jesus refused to separate from unsavory people. In the incarnation, Jesus joined human society in all its corruption.

Clearly, if Obadiah could work for Ahab and Joseph could work for Pharaoh, believers *may* work almost anywhere, if they can do good, or at least restrain evil, there. Other heroes of the faith did the same thing. Daniel was a trusted advisor for notoriously cruel Babylonian kings (Dan. 1–6), Ezra and Nehemiah were high officials in Persia (Ezra 7:1; Neh. 2:1–8; 5:14), and Esther served God at great risk in Xerxes' palace (Esth. 1–9).

Esther reminds us that believers don't necessarily choose their tasks. She didn't volunteer for a beauty contest; the king *ordered* his officials to "gather all the beautiful young virgins" and she "*was taken* into the king's palace" (Esth. 2:2–8). Later, Esther risked everything for her people. As Mordecai, her uncle, told her, "Who knows whether you have not" become queen "for such a time as this?" (4:14). Similarly, Joseph came to leadership when his brothers sold him into slavery, and Daniel started life in Babylon as a war captive. We never know when God may appoint us to dangerous but strategic service.

We need a sober optimism about such service. When national or local governments produce foolish policies, disheartened

Christians wonder if it is even possible to serve with integrity in politics. Joseph, Obadiah, Daniel, and Esther all say yes. Yet, as realists, we must also say no on occasion. Moses refused to serve a genocidal pharaoh. Daniel served Nebuchadnezzar, but it almost cost him his life, and others did take a stand and perish for it (Dan. 3:1–30; 6:4–24; Heb. 11:33–37).

Principles for Working in Difficult Places

The world needs disciples to labor in every industry where sin and corruption thrive. But we need to watch for self-deception. If we taste success, the pressure to fit within a corrupt culture mounts. People then find ways to justify their decision to stay in a position that grants them wealth, influence, or security. To prevent compromises, we must question ourselves:

- Am I serving my King? Promoting justice? Or fitting in and make a living?
- When potential conflicts between business and kingdom goals arise, do I stand on principle or do what it takes to keep my job? Am I willing to begin and endure conflict for a good cause?
- What motivates me? The opinions of others? Wealth? Love for God and neighbor?
- Do I collaborate with fellow believers to achieve godly goals?

In Paul's terms, we need to transform this age, not conform to it (Rom. 12:1–2). Again, we will avoid illegal activity. In marginal cases, we will consider what to do if the situation grows worse instead of improving. A special challenge lies with business activities that are legal and profitable, but immoral. Certain enterprises target those very activities. In my view, disciples should never promote gambling. We might produce wine, if our convictions allow it, but not the cheap beer, gin, and whiskey that is marketed to heavy drinkers and that fuels drunkenness. We must also allow for advances in knowledge to reshape business activities. Eighty year ago, asbestos and tobacco were considered harmless. But once a risk is known, disciples should be the first to promote safety. In general terms, we should serve God, restrain evil, and advance love, justice, and mercy at work. We can't simply follow orders. We are God's agents and must promote his reign and values. Consider the darker side of the automotive world as a case study.

Each year pollsters publish lists of America's most and least respected occupations. The heroes are familiar: nurses, doctors, and teachers. The villains are too: lawyers, gun dealers, journalists, politicians, used-car salesmen. The rankings hurt since many of the villains are skilled, dedicated folk who toil in professions that lost their way. Others, like car salesmen, have had poor ratings for years.

I once needed a used car and visited a dealer with a good reputation. A receptionist pointed me toward John, who lit up, shouting and gesticulating, when I told him my oldest daughter needed a car for college. "I got a car on a trade-in just yesterday. A couple hicks had money from an insurance settlement, and it was burning a hole in their pockets. I sold them a new vehicle and positively *stole* their old car from them, so I can offer you quite a deal."

I thought, "Who starts a sale by bragging that he steals from his customers?" I could have walked away, but I'd taken my daughter with me. Seeing an educational opportunity, I tried to start a Socratic dialogue while standing on hot pavement. "You say you *stole* this car from a fool yesterday, so you can offer me a great deal today?"

He grinned wolfishly. "That's right!"

"But if you stole it from a customer *yesterday*, and I'm a customer, what might you want to do to me *today*?"

He looked at me with blank incomprehension. I tried again. "You admit that you stole a car from two suckers yesterday, but what if you decide *I'm* a sucker too?" The blank look deepened, and I tried one more time until he blurted, "Look, do you want to buy this car or not?" Here was a man so accustomed to his own braggadocio and deceit that he couldn't hear himself confess to thievery. How I longed for an honest salesman!

Used-car salesmen face intense pressure to reach monthly sales quotas and industry structures seem to promote dishonesty. Still, people need cars. What should an honest car salesman do? Abandon the field and sell appliances? Not necessarily. Operating like Obadiah or Joseph, a man could build clientele through a reputation for honesty, even when working for a questionable firm. Or a reformer could create a new model: full information and guaranteed quality at slightly higher prices. In fact, that very model has recently found success in several cities. If it spreads and is profitable, it could slowly transform the used-car market.

This chapter has argued that believers are free to work for godless leaders in daunting environments, if they are prepared to be faithful. We began with individuals, Mike the CFO and Lisa the engineer, making tough business decisions, and moved to Joseph and Obadiah, leaders who served wicked kings. All four made courageous moral choices. But if we revisit their stories, we notice that they didn't just make a strong decision in a crisis; they also protected others. Mike helped the people in his firm avoid involvement with pornography, and Obadiah spared the prophets so they could fulfill their callings when Ahab was gone. Of course, we realize that it's possible take a bold stand, lose the battle, and then forfeit our jobs as a result. The great matter is to be faithful, to seek first the kingdom, and to trust the King to care for us. He does not leave his people defenseless (Ps. 37:25).

At best, leaders inspire their followers to help them establish an order that widens the path to justice. Then the right decisions are obvious and repeatable, not isolated and risky. Society needs people with gifts, vision, passion, boldness, and allies to bring reform. They are willing to fail and start over. But they keep trying to restructure their part of the world so people can flourish. Reform is often the work of the young, the energetic, and the optimistic. When cares and salaries increase, the pressure to conform increases as people strive for influence and affluence. But mature adults can lead reforms if they can control their interest in wealth and security. So let us hear the call to work in dark places and labor to bring them into the light.

Discussion Questions

1. When have you faced a moral conflict at work? Describe the situation and your response. What did you do right? What might you have done better?
2. How could Obadiah serve Ahab? How could Daniel serve Nebuchadnezzar? Are you the kind of person who could mitigate evil by working in a hard place?
3. Review the "basic principles" section. Are you following the basics for disciples who toil in difficult situations?
4. Review the chapter's diagnostic questions: Are you serving your King? Or fitting in and make a living? When conflicts between business and kingdom goals arise, do you follow God's way or do what it takes to keep your job?
5. What motivates you at work? The opinions of others? Wealth? Love for God and neighbor?
6. Do you collaborate with fellow believers to achieve godly goals?

8

WORK, REST, AND THE
RHYTHMS OF LIFE

Savoring Rest

Since last summer, my granddaughter Estelle, then nearly four, has been teaching me about time. On Fridays, she arrives at 7 A.M., accompanied by her mother and baby brother, Jonah. After a few minutes spying birds through a kitchen window, we might play a game like Blockhead or shape our hands to resemble friendly dinosaurs before we sit down for our little breakfast club. Afterward, Estelle chooses a park nearby and we head out while Jonah naps. One park features cascading streams, bridges, interactive sculptures, boulders that are perfect for little climbers, and a lake stocked with hungry fish. After we arrive, Estelle typically leads as we hop down a flight of steps that takes us to a gurgling, insect-laden stream. After checking the stream and the nearby blackberry bushes, we reach a sculpture of a girl running. She shouts, "Let's go feed the fish!" and sprints ahead, heels flying. After the fish, we head for a course of rocks, which she climbs because their crevices shelter flowers, bees, and dragonflies. She watches them in wonder, even though it slows our journey toward our stated objective, which is to run around the sculptures a quarter mile ahead. On higher rocks, Estelle reaches for my hand, but she holds on after the danger has passed, so far as I can tell, because it feels warm. We may name the flowers and insects or launch a tiny raft on the water. By 9:30, whatever the delights of the hour, I am itching for the tasks of the day, because decades of devotion to goals and efficiency have shaped me. But Estelle is teaching me that relationships need timelessness, not efficiency. I turn off my phone, hoping to silence the ticking in my mind. I wonder if time will stop in the New Creation, or if it will become a quiet friend, a term that labels sequences—this happened before that—but nothing more.[1] Walking with Estelle, I realize that whatever else happens to time, it will surely cease to be a foe that marches us toward decrepitude and death and presses us to *accomplish more* while strength remains.

My story is common, at least among people who live in cultures dominated by clocks and efficiency. As we race to finish self-assigned tasks, time tracks our success. Other cultures construe time differently. Before people measured time with clocks and divided it into discrete packets, they rose with the sun; marked morning, midday, afternoon, and sunset; and stopped working at dusk. Time was a river, not a weight. People floated down the river, which gently carried them downstream.

Clocks allow people to think about time in units, packages, or slivers—seconds, minutes, hours. Clocks make time seem like a fixed quantity. We only have so many hours in a day, so we need to manage it, save it, measure it. This mentality may move us to get more done, but it drives and harries us. Leisure seems like a waste. Relaxation doesn't put money in our wallets or add a nickel to the gross national product. The contemporary view of time allows efficiency to become a demigod. If someone asks, "How was your day?" we reply, "Good! I got a lot done."

This view of time hides an essential truth: while we say we *save* time and *make* time, we do neither. Judged by the clock, every minute is identical. But God says there are crucial moments and

---

1. Philosophers have long debated whether time is an objective, independent entity, like space, or whether it is merely a label for the sequence of events.

that we should make "the most of every opportunity, because the days are evil" (Eph. 5:16 NIV, 1984 version). If time *is* a demigod, it feels like a hostile deity. We want to savor joyful moments and slow time down. We want the last ski run, the last laugh over dessert, and the rosy sunset to continue forever, but they slip away. But the Lord God is the Master of time, seasons (Gen. 8:22), calendars, and everyone's time on earth: "The length of our days is seventy years—or eighty, if we have the strength; yet their span is but trouble and sorrow, for they quickly pass, and we fly away . . . Teach us to number our days aright, that we may gain a heart of wisdom" (Ps. 90:10, 12 NIV, 1984 version).

Many resist the whip of efficiency, the pressure for ceaseless productivity. Some seek work that allows more leisure. The God-given rhythm of life both corrects laziness and offers relief to those who feel pressure to be industrious at all times. The Lord teaches us to work, then pause to sleep, eat, pray, and rest each week.

Creation and Rhythm

In the beginning, there was work, then rest, for God created, then paused to review what he had done (Gen. 1:1–2:3). Since God created us in his image, that is our pattern too. We should work, then reflect on our toil and, ideally, call it "good." Unfortunately, many are prone to work, then work more. Others work too little, perhaps because they cannot find suitable employment or because they are slugs. As fallen creatures, we typically work too much or too little, so we need to consider God's ways.

When the Lord created the universe, Ronald Wallace observes, he lavished his "boundless skill, energy, and inventiveness" on it. Yet he did not wholly immerse himself in his work, he held something back. He detached himself from creation, so that we can distinguish God's work from God himself. There is more to God than his work product. At the end of each day of creation, he "pauses, stands back, collects himself," and then judges his accomplishment "good." The labor of creation did not "exhaust

Him or bind Him" to the world.[2] Pantheists, by contrast, propose that God is so fused with the world that the world *is* God. But after six days of creation, God chose to rest and assess his accomplishment. We should rest and evaluate too, for we are more than our work, just as he is.

Astronomers estimate that there are 2 x 10 to the twenty-third power stars in the universe. To get a sense of that, imagine that every person who ever lived—roughly one hundred billion people according to demographic estimates—named stars for sixty hours per week for sixty years, at a rate of five stars per minute. At that prodigious rate, everyone would need a thousand lifetimes to name the stars. But even in that incandescent creative act, the Lord remained distinct from his work.

Jesus followed a similar pattern. He loved his work and gave tireless, concentrated energy to it. Once, when he was tired and hungry, his disciples urged him to eat. He replied, "My food is to do the will of him who sent me and to finish his work" (John 4:34 NIV); that is, he loves his work, so that even when it is tiring, it nourishes his spirit (Eccl. 2:24–25). Before he gave up his spirit on the cross, he exulted, "It is finished," for he was satisfied with his work (John 19:30; cf. Isa. 53:11). Despite his love for work, Jesus also stopped to pray, sleep, share a meal, strike up conversations, and worship, and so should we. No matter how fulfilling our labor, God designed people for more than work.

Specifically, we refrain from work on the Sabbath because the Lord "rested on the seventh day" (Ex. 20:10–11). Like the Lord, we should work enthusiastically, but we should also know when to stop.

Fall: Work and Overwork

Professionals, business leaders, engineers, and artisans rightly consider the most efficient use of time, space, and capital.

---

2. Ronald Wallace, *The Ten Commandments: A Study of Ethical Freedom* (Grand Rapids: Eerdmans, 1965), 65–66.

Productivity is good! To waste time and talent is to squander God's gifts. Time, skill, and materials are scarce. Farmers must work when it is time to plant and harvest (Prov. 10:4–5; 20:4). Wealth should be preserved (Prov. 29:3; Luke 16:1). Again, the godly should act at the opportune moment (Eph. 5:15–16).

That said, we must not read the Western passion for efficiency into Scripture. After all, when God created humans, he gave us a need for sleep and rest. We are not sharks that must keep moving lest they die. In addition to the sleep God grants every night, he ordains an entire day of rest. That creates about seventy "nonproductive" hours per week, if anyone is counting. Furthermore, God doesn't seem to *hurry* as we do. His covenants unfold over centuries.

Professionals are often slow to discover these principles. Or, rather, we acknowledge them intellectually but not experientially. Work becomes a bully that shoves everything else aside. Kristin van Ogtrop, once the editor of the magazines *Glamour* and *Real Simple*, lamented the tyranny of work when she was a young mother:

> I will never be able to share the surprise [my kids] feel when they find a cicada in the grass, because stopping to marvel at the cicada means I will miss my morning train. . . . I will long for a time when I will never yell at my kids just because I am late. . . . Because before I know it, my boys will be grown. . . . Four little feet jumping on the bed will be a distant memory. And things like cicadas will have lost their magic, and my children will be gone for good.[3]

Van Ogtrop labels the problem well, but feels powerless to change it because she chained herself to her career. That is the plight of the professional working mother. Cutting back on the

---

3. Kristin van Ogtrop, "Attila the Honey I'm Home," in *Bitch in the House: 26 Women Tell the Truth about Sex, Solitude, Work, Motherhood, and Marriage,* ed. Cathi Hanauer (New York: HarperCollins, 2002), 169.

schedule feels like a career-suicide. Moreover, talented women who stay at home to raise children—a rewarding and grueling calling—endure criticism for not working or for failing to fulfill their potential. American culture admires the drive to make a mark at work, even though that drive often fosters self-destructive obsessions, as great innovators like Thomas Edison and Steve Jobs show.

Overwork and Underemployment

Overwork is especially tempting for adults who believe in their work. Reasons for overwork can be assigned to two categories: (1) the structural or objective and (2) the personal or subjective. Structural reasons for overwork reflect the job market. First, longer hours generally bring more pay. Additional income is *desirable* for the middle class but *essential* to millions with jobs that don't pay a living wage. At minimum wage, two or three jobs are necessary for survival. Second, many employers prefer to have fewer employees who work longer hours. Employers can save money on benefits if they have four employees working fifty hours per week instead of five working forty hours. Third, the decline of job security creates incentives for overload. In theory, constant corporate restructuring and the rise of temporary workers make every laborer expendable. In that environment, no one wants to look like a weak link. Meanwhile, the wise keep building skills and networks to prepare for the next shift in the job market. And the constant pressure of competitive markets becomes the drums driving the pace.

Personal or internal reasons for overwork reflect lifestyle choices. We work to excess in order to buy premium products, services, and experiences. One financial decision leads to another. If we buy a grand home, we will then need suitable furnishings, landscaping, and insurance. Each financial commitment carries financial pressure. Pride and ego also motivate overwork, since luxurious cars and exotic vacations project success. Finally, dedication to a cause that is understaffed can propel overwork. This may especially tempt those who love the Lord, but forget that he can accomplish his goals without them.

Meanwhile, millions wish they could work more, but can only find part-time work. Surviving on several part-time jobs or one-time gigs, they long for full-time jobs that pay well. So deliberate overwork is hardly the only problem.

Sadly, believers often conform to culture instead of questioning it. A prominent Christian once told his harried readers they just needed to sleep less. To pray more, he declared, set the alarm fifteen minutes earlier. To accomplish more, set it earlier still. Your body will get used to it, he promised. This may be good counsel for sluggards, but for workaholics, it's like urging rock climbers to sleep on a cliff overnight. The harvest of chronic sleep deprivation is moodiness, loss of focus, and addiction to stimulants. When members of that tribe collapse at the desk, they use confessional language: *"I'll admit* that I took a nap." People used to say, "When I relax, I feel guilty." Now they feel guilty for getting adequate sleep. The result? We lose half of the afternoon because we are too tired to concentrate. The bed beckons as exhaustion arrives in the evening, but we convince ourselves we need to do four things first.

Why do we do this to ourselves? Because the boss wants a reply, because failure is not an option, because we feel guilty for playing computer games in the afternoon, when we were so weary. The same sensibility coaxes us to work on Sunday afternoon: we want to shrink the to-do list, and while that may relieve pressure for the coming week, it's painful to wake up weary on Monday morning.

The Day of Rest—Principles and Practices

God's law, grounded in his work in creation and redemption, cuts through our bad habits with bracing simplicity:

> Observe the Sabbath day, to keep it holy, as the LORD your God commanded you. Six days you shall labor and do all your work,

but the seventh day is a Sabbath to the LORD your God. On it you shall not do any work, you or your son or your daughter or your male servant or your female servant, or your ox or your donkey or any of your livestock, or the sojourner who is within your gates, that your male servant and your female servant may rest as well as you. You shall remember that you were a slave in the land of Egypt, and the LORD your God brought you out from there with a mighty hand and an outstretched arm. Therefore the LORD your God commanded you to keep the Sabbath day. (Deut. 5:12–15)

The law suits both idlers and overachievers. The lazy need to work six days, while fanatics need to rest one day. Notice that the law is *social*. Neither the master *nor his servants* shall work. The law protects the sojourner, the outsider, the powerless. In this it surpasses other ancient law codes. The Code of Hammurabi had one set of laws for free men with property and another for everyone else. The Greeks typically viewed slaves as inferior humans: no rest for them. But God's law protects everyone. In that spirit, leaders today must ensure that their people find rest.

Notice that Moses' law names a Sabbath *day*. Likewise the New Testament speaks of the Lord's Day. Thus, the Lord ordains a *day* of rest, not an hour or two for worship. In Exodus 20, the accent falls on rest. In Deuteronomy 5, when Moses restates the law, he focuses on redemption: "Remember that you were a slave in the land of Egypt, and the LORD your God brought you out from there with a mighty hand.... Therefore the LORD your God commanded you to keep the Sabbath day" (Deut. 5:15). The early church gathered "on the first day of every week" (1 Cor. 16:2; cf. Acts 20:7), so it is the norm for believers to gather on Sundays to worship and then to rest.

Disciples wonder how to practice this, since childcare and food preparation are inescapable. Workaholics try to drag their coworkers into their web, and technological societies rely on systems that provide power, water, transportation, medical care, and more. While the pace of labor typically slows on Saturday and Sunday, it seems impossible for laborers in certain sectors to escape work.

What should a disciple do? Jesus may have the answer. In his era, Sabbath regulations became minutely detailed. Israelites could write on the Sabbath—if the word had just two letters. They could walk—up to 0.6 miles. They could prepare food—if it was less than a gulp. A physician could heal, provided the patient would die that day without treatment. Jesus ignored these man-made rules.

The Gospels mention the Sabbath about fifty times. A few instances simply name the day of the week,[4] but in most cases, Jewish leaders falsely accuse Jesus of violating the Sabbath, by healing the sick, for example (Luke 6:1–9; 13:10–16; 14:1–15; John 5:9–18; 9:14–16). In an episode reported in Matthew 12:1–8, Mark 2:23–28, and Luke 6:1–5, Pharisees criticize Jesus for *harvesting* on the Sabbath when Jesus and his disciples plucked heads of grain from roadside fields (which the law allowed) and popped them in their mouths. When Jesus corrected the Pharisees, he also explained the Sabbath.

First, Jesus announces, "I desire mercy, not sacrifice." Generally, this means it is better to live God's way by showing mercy than to offer a sacrifice for failing to do so. The application is that Jesus correctly let his disciples meet their need for food—showing mercy to them—instead of hurting them by following the prevailing interpretation of the law. Therefore, Jesus forbids Sabbath rules that make the day a burden.

Second, Jesus states, "The Sabbath was made for man, not man for the Sabbath" (Mark 2:27). That is, God designed the Sabbath for the flourishing of humanity. Sabbath rules should remember that. Third, "The Son of Man is lord even of the Sabbath" (Mark 2:28; Matt. 12:8). As Lord, Jesus will settle the Sabbath

---

4. See Matthew 28:1; Mark 1:21; 16:1; Luke 4:16.

rules. Paul agrees that believers should not condemn one another's Sabbath practices (Col. 2:16; cf. Rom. 14:4–5). The law serves mankind, so the Sabbath should bring joy and restoration, not burdens. When Jesus healed on the Sabbath, he demonstrated that. Acts of mercy belong to the Sabbath. So the day promotes rest, worship, prayer, and acts of mercy.

There is also room for recreation. John Calvin, hardly a careless man, enjoyed lawn bowling after he preached on Sundays. The Canons of Dort say the day is for worship, rest from work, acts of charity, and necessities. And it only forbids "those recreations which impede the worship of God."[5] The Puritans were more restrictive, insisting that the Lord's Day be given wholly to worship, prayer, Scripture, charity, and rest. Westminster's catechisms expressly forbid "such . . . recreations as are lawful on other days" and "profaning the day by idleness."[6] Strictly speaking, this statement calls rest itself into question.

In shunning Sabbath regulations, both Jesus and Paul let believers discover the best way to use the day, beyond worship and discipleship. That permits shared meals that include a discussion of the issues of the hour. We can visit the sick or the lonely. We may read, tell stories, call friends, and take a nap. We might walk through the woods and celebrate God's creation.

Because the Sabbath principle challenges Western practices and perspectives, we create excuses for working and so deprive ourselves of rest. In the Western mind, we work five days to earn the right to rest and play on the week*end*. But God tells believers

5. R. Scott Clark, trans., "The Synod of Dort on Sabbath Observance," session 164, article VI, from H. H. Kuyper, *De Post-Acta of Nahandelingen van de nationale Synode van Dordrecht in 1618 en 1619 gehouden een Historische Studie* (Amsterdam, 1899), 184–86, http://rscottclark.org/2012/08/the-synod-of-dort-on-sabbath-observance. The Heidelberg Catechism, question 103, offers believers a similar freedom.

6. Westminster Confession of Faith, 21; Westminster Shorter Catechism, 60–61; Westminster Larger Catechism, 117, 119. Westminster Shorter Catechism, 60, teaches that the "whole" day should be devoted to worship and "works of necessity and mercy," but does not mention rest. The Westminster Confession of Faith, 21:7, forbids that believers even think about recreation on the Sabbath.

to *start* the week with rest *before* we work. In Scripture, rest is a gift, not a reward.

Sunday recreation is more controversial. The love of sports often leads Christians to forfeit worship by attending events or by competing. Still, the Lord's Day can include the right kind of physical activity. Almost everyone approves of a Sunday walk, but disciples who are fit can run or ride a bicycle as easily as others walk. For athletes, light exercise is restorative and joyful.

The Canons of Dort forbid recreations that impede worship but do not forbid *all* recreation. Sports tournaments and leagues dominate Sunday schedules and obstruct corporate worship, but casual play can be godly. Play, like worship and rest, is an activity of abundance. Children can play because they trust that their parents meet their needs. Likewise, believing adults can rest and play because we have a Father in heaven. When a father plays with his children on Sundays, he shows that he trusts God to provide for him, so he need not work perpetually.

So the right kind of play fits the Lord's Day. On Sundays, parents and children can frolic together in the water or play hide-and-seek or throw a frisbee. Older children might ride bicycles or play casual sports with the family.

This will unnerve certain Christians who wonder how far I intend to ride or how hard I will throw a ball. Romans 14, which touches controversial topics, including Sabbath observance, applies here. Paul warns Christians not to despise or condemn one another in areas where informed disciples sincerely disagree (Rom. 14:3–4). He concludes: "One person esteems one day as better than another, while another esteems all days alike. Each one should be fully convinced in his own mind" (v. 5). Each person should examine the issue, then decide how to observe the Lord's Day, without condemning fellow believers who worship and rest a bit differently.

When I grew up, men dropped athletics before they were forty, so I thank the Lord I could still run, hike, work out, and play basketball and tennis in my forties, fifties, and sixties. I still play tennis competitively from Monday to Saturday; on Sundays I play casually, but not competitively. For me, the need to focus on every point, to win matches, clashes with genuine rest. But I will hit tennis balls on Sunday with family or friends who enjoy a bit of exercise on the court and then friendly conversation. For me, *restful* tennis means no one keeps score. Restful tennis makes me thankful and relaxed. I also take long walks with my wife or go for a gentle jog with my dog on the Lord's Day. My approach will puzzle some but make sense to those who delight in physical activity and find it restful. Worship, rest, and Christian fellowship are given. After that there are options. Let each person form their convictions and practice them (Rom. 14:5).

The Sabbath, Rest, and Western Culture

The Sabbath principle challenges Western practices. Americans think the work week entitles them to do whatever they wish on the *weekend*, while insisting that employees are accessible, if needed. But we don't earn leisure by working hard. The Lord God raised Jesus from the dead and set aside the resurrection day to celebrate that. In the secular mind, Sunday is the back half of the weekend, a day to sleep in, shop, read the paper, or putter in the garden. For athletes, Sunday is sports day. For travelers, it's the day to return from trips. For certain folk, Sunday means less work, not rest. They make a few calls, find some information. So the culture makes it easy to abandon the day of rest.

Thinking socially, teachers should not assign work that is due Monday morning. Parents must not program children's activities to fill Sundays. If the Lord, the Creator, rested, then so should we. But Western culture presents many obstacles.

Technological societies cannot offer a universal day of rest. The power grid, hospitals, and airports must hum along and robots never sleep. So the work rolls on, because efficiency demands it. Believers resist all this. Christian business leaders shape their work to give people a day of rest. Pastors can help them explore the best way to apply the Sabbath principle in their field. For their part, employees should state that they worship on Sundays, except for emergencies. Ideally, we become indispensable so that leaders gladly accommodate our faith.

This is no small challenge. In retail, Sunday is a good day for revenue. To close is to forfeit revenue, but also to honor God and care for employees. The "Closed on Sunday" sign testifies that owners trust God to provide, that they believe God gives his law "for our good" (Deut. 10:13). Restaurants show the value of a day of rest. Restaurant work is demanding and the late hours disrupt normal routines. A day off calms the spirit and restores order. It guarantees that no matter how many shift swaps occur, no one works fourteen consecutive days. But decision points aren't so clear in other enterprises. When do medical or security personnel really need to be called in? If the communication industry never sleeps, can it at least slow down?

Business leaders should be honest with interviewees about the time demands a job imposes. It is insufficient to comment, "There could be a little work on weekends." Remember that the fourth commandment tells Israel's masters to give rest to their servants. That is, they create an environment where everyone rests. Good masters and employers make it easy for servants and employees to obey God. Managers should take special interest in workers with few skills or low mobility. They cannot negotiate from a position of strength, so they are easily exploited and their immobility makes it hard to escape; female workers who endure sexual harassment to keep a good job are a special case of a common situation.

For employer and employee alike, to rest one day in seven is to live by faith. Resting resembles tithing. Both are symbolic acts and confessions of faith. They say, "We can accomplish more in six days with His favor than in seven days without it." By resting, we confess that we can prosper without tireless toil. Both the Sabbath and the tithe address workaholics and worriers who think they need to work and plan forever, whether due to greed or worry. But experience teaches that we can initiate every plan and watch it come to naught. Yet when God grants his favor, we hardly do anything and we meet success.

Living by Faith (and Dethroning Work as a Demigod)

Moses warns Israel, "Do not follow the crowd in doing wrong" (Ex. 23:2 NIV). But we readily follow the crowd into overwork, since work is a seductive deity. "Serve me," it promises, "and I will give you security, respect, and wealth." The gospel uproots the motives for overwork. It offers the security of God's family, the wealth and status of his heirs. It teaches us that we cannot *earn* the great prize, a place in God's kingdom, because it is both gift and inheritance (Ps. 37:9–11; Matt. 5:5; Eph. 2:1–9). God says, "I have loved you with an everlasting love," and that brings assurances that no work can match (Jer. 31:3).

In the opening chapter, I mentioned that my father told me, again and again, that I was lazy, good for nothing, and always would be. That spurred a long, futile attempt to prove him wrong. My experience is hardly unique. If you heard, "You'll never amount to anything," the Lord says, "My love for you is gracious. You cannot *do* anything to prove yourself lovable or worthy. And yet, I do prepare good works for you to do" (see Eph. 2:8). If someone called you weak, Jesus says, "My power is made perfect in weakness." With Paul we can say, "When I am weak, then I am strong" (2 Cor. 12:9–10).

The gospel heals or defangs work as a compulsive quest for worth and wealth. Besides, whatever we have of these, they never satisfy, since someone always has more. As a god, work lies when it promises wealth and happiness. Solomon knew better: "He who loves money will not be satisfied with money. . . . Sweet is the sleep of a laborer" (Eccl. 5:10–12). To be sure, there are times for exceptional toil, but we justify neglect of the Sabbath far too easily, to our harm.[7] I worked too hard for years, but eventually

---

7. Some employers gladly exploit employees with an excessive appetite for work by assigning them urgent tasks.

I wore out. Now I take the day of rest seriously. That manifests itself in mornings with my grandchildren, but the source is rest in the gospel and assurance that the Lord will accomplish all that he determines to do, with or without my aid (Isa. 46:9–11).[8]

So let us work hard enough, then pray with Moses, "Let the favor of the Lord our God be upon us, and establish the work of our hands upon us; yes, establish the work of our hands!" (Ps. 90:17). And let us hear Solomon's comfort, "Unless the LORD builds the house, those who build it labor in vain. . . . It is in vain that you rise up early and go late to rest, eating the bread of anxious toil, for he gives to his beloved sleep" (Ps. 127:1–2). We can stop working and go to sleep because God cares for us *while* we sleep. So we can rest each night and take an entire day for rest each week, content that we labored faithfully and that our labor is not in vain (1 Cor. 15:58).

Discussion Questions

1. Do you rest from your ordinary labor one day each week? Why or why not?
2. What keeps you from following God's pattern for rest and work? Do you experience *external* pressure to work on the day of rest? Do you resist it? How? Or are *you* the main impediment? How do you pressure yourself to work, even when you could rest? Do you resist that pressure? How?
3. Do you find or make time for spiritual rest—to rest in the work of Christ and his gospel? Share what happens when you make time to rest physically and spiritually.
4. How does our culture typically view Sunday? How do you view Sunday? How does the Lord want you to spend the Lord's Day?
5. Why is it so hard for some of us to stop working one day a week, or even to stop working and go to sleep?

8. Tim Keller, *Every Good Endeavor* (New York: Penguin, 2012), 125–50.

PART 3

REFORMATION

9

THE ROOTS OF
REFORMATIONS AT WORK

Social Reform as the Spontaneous Fruit of Faith

The next two chapters propose both a *theology* and a *plan* for social reform through work. We will see how believers' spontaneous acts can lead to lasting change. Indeed, it seems that most reforms begin spontaneously, almost accidentally. When our eyes are open, we see ways to do justice or show love in our callings. This is a response to God's prior love. "We love because he first loved us" (1 John 4:19). We love because "God's love has been poured into our hearts" (Rom. 5:5). These acts can't earn God's favor, but they do respond rightly to it. Paul says believers are "created in Christ Jesus for good works, which God prepared beforehand, that we should walk in them" (Eph. 2:10). Both Jesus and Paul call good deeds "fruit" to convey that they are the natural result of faith. Healthy trees cannot help but bear fruit (Matt. 7:17–19; John 15:1–16; Rom. 7:4–6).

That is how Rebecca Green (chap. 3) reformed her school library. She expelled books that seemed detrimental to her students. Eventually, she developed a list of criteria for her decisions, and they became school policy. But if Rebecca publishes her criteria, she might initiate a movement. In this way, a few of our innumerable acts of justice and mercy become a movement and gain a formal standing.

Christians act spontaneously, but leaders are also accountable to make plans. They see that their abilities, position, and allies grant the ability to effect systemic change. They believe they have the gifts of leadership and the best possess godly zeal for it (Rom. 12:8). Jesus says, "Much is required from those to whom much is given" (Luke 12:48 NLT). This saying follows a parable where Jesus describes a farmer whose land is so productive that he has no space for all his crops. He decides to indulge himself, to "eat, drink, [and] be merry" (v. 19). But tomorrow he dies! God says, "Fool! This night your soul is *required* of you" (v. 21). He will then render an account of his life. The term *required* is interesting. It translates the verb *apaiteō*, which normally means to ask or demand that something—often a loan—be returned.[1] The idea, therefore, is that life itself, with all its privileges, is a loan from God. Everyone will render an account for their use of the resources God entrusts to them. That includes their training, expertise, and positions of authority and influence, not just wealth.

Isaiah 32:1–8 describes the strategic importance of strong leaders in poetry:

> Behold, a king will reign in righteousness,
>   and princes will rule in justice.
> Each will be like a hiding place from the wind,
>   a shelter from the storm,
> like streams of water in a dry place,
>   like the shade of a great rock in a weary land.
> Then the eyes of those who see will not be closed,
>   and the ears of those who hear will give attention.
> The heart of the hasty will understand and know,

---

1. This is the definition in standard Greek lexicons. The idea that life is a loan from God is explicit in Wisdom, the popular noncanonical Jewish book, which says that a human being lives "a little while" and then "is required to return the soul that was lent him" (15:8). Luke 12:20 reflects this. See Craig Keener, *The IVP Bible Background Commentary: New Testament* (Downers Grove, IL: InterVarsity, 1993), 224.

and the tongue of the stammerers will hasten to speak
distinctly.
The fool will no more be called noble,
nor the scoundrel said to be honorable . . .
But he who is noble plans noble things,
and on noble things he stands.

This prophecy foretells the reign of a righteous king who
will restore Israel. Ultimately, Jesus is this King. Under the
righteous king, Isaiah says, "princes will rule in justice." This
describes the noble sons of Israel's kings, but it also applies to
any prince or ruler who effectuates the reign of Jesus in a sphere
they oversee. When they lead, under King Jesus, everyone finds
shelters beneath them from life's storms, and there the thirsty
find water (32:2). The world—at least their part of it—begins to
change as people start to see, hear, and understand (vv. 3–4).
Corrupt societies invert God's values. The powerful delight in
their ability to rob the weak. The worst entertainments are both
witless and degrading. When the king and his princes stop that,
people recognize fools and scoundrels for what they are (v. 5).
Rulers make noble plans and they stand (v. 8). This vision for
the blessed results of Christ's reign should motivate all whom
God calls to princely rule.

Among North American believers, the propensity to individualism can blind us to opportunities to lead. We instinctively
think we do good at work in private, solo acts: speaking the truth,
helping needy colaborers, and sharing the gospel when we can.
But we forget that we can love battalions of neighbors, far and
near, through the long reach of our work. For example, if we work
in the food industry, we think we love our neighbors by bringing
meals to the sick and contributing to food pantries. These acts
are good, but food workers love far more people by laboring in
farms, grocery stores, and restaurants. When we develop hardy
and productive plants that consume fewer resources, when we
grow nutritious food, transport it well, and sell it at a fair price,

we love neighbors everywhere. Likewise, a craftsman loves *neighbors* yet unborn when he makes sturdy, comfortable chairs that last for centuries.

At work, we have the most skill and training, the most resources, and the strongest teams, so we multiply our capacity to love people.[2] Therefore, if anyone changes the world, they probably do so at work, whether spontaneously or deliberately. Let's consider how that can happen in medicine.

The Spontaneous Social Reform of Clay Porter[3]

Clay Porter is a cancer researcher and physician whose pioneering methods of surgery have saved the lives of many patients with soft tissue cancers. Porter has published scholarly papers, held a chair at a prestigious research hospital, trained dozens of residents, and traveled the world to demonstrate his methods at surgical centers.

After decades as a surgeon, Porter began to focus on postoperative cancer survivors. Because he specialized in sensitive tissue cancers, he saw the devastating effects of certain pre- and postsurgical treatments. Patients could be cancer free and functioning normally after surgery, Porter found, "only to lose that function due to the toxicity of additional treatments." Combined radiation and chemotherapy could destroy breathing when targeting the chest. It could damage saliva glands and throat muscles, dooming survivors to a dry mouth and permanent difficulties in swallowing and speaking.

As Porter considered the effects of additional radiation and chemotherapy on patients, he decided to investigate a question: How many lives do extra treatments save when applied to critical soft tissues? How often does it prevent cancer from recurring?

---

2. Lester DeKoster, *Work: The Meaning of Your Life* (Grand Rapids: Christian Library Press, 1982).

3. I changed the name and certain details in this story to protect the physician's privacy. I have also drawn on interviews with other physicians in extrapolating lessons from this research.

If the prophylactic value is low, might people trade a slightly elevated risk that a cancer would return to keep vital organs working well?

It can be controversial to ask such questions. Is it ethical to invite patients to decrease or eliminate extra therapy to improve the quality of their life? Suppose their prognosis were excellent. Is it responsible to offer tradeoffs such as, "Your saliva glands and vocal cords will work better, but the chance of cancer returning will rise"?

A trial of Porter's proposals might lead standards of care to change. If there were less treatment, that would mean fewer patients and fewer trials for other physicians. Revenues from both clinical care and research trials might be lost. If certain treatments were no longer standard, specialists might see a drop in the need for their services. In the academic side of medicine, commercially based clinical trial funding derived from large pharmaceutical and medical technology firms could decrease. And what if Porter found that the death rate would increase by 2 percent and that patients still wanted to skip extra treatments? Could hospitals ethically allow patients to risk death in exchange for a higher quality of life?

Because he questioned accepted medical procedures, because he stepped into the realms of other experts, and because his work threatened financial upheaval, Porter faced opposition. This is typical. Reformers must expect opposition from those who are well served by the status quo. In large institutions, reformers need determination to fight through inertia, but they also need allies in positions of authority. Eventually, Porter saw that he did not have enough allies to continue his research unimpeded, so he transferred to a hospital that fully supported his work. From there, he continued his research and created protocols that improved the life of cancer survivors. Over time, large studies from other centers and national databases corroborated his work.

Dr. Porter's proposals proceed from careful scientific

observation of numerous patients, but his faith shapes his work. First, he loves his patients and wants the best possible life for them. Second, he believes, and has seen through study and observation, that God designed the body to heal itself *and* to combat cancer via the immune system, which high doses of radiation and chemotherapy can compromise. Third, biblical ethics instruct him to report his findings honestly and rigorously, without stretching the data to make his case and without bowing to political or economic pressure to minimize unsettling findings.

Fourth, as a believer, he holds that preventing physical death is not the sole measure of successful medical treatment. Physicians know that a time comes to stop treatment and let a patient die, even if they decide cases differently. Suppose a physician pushes on this minimal consensus: "There is a time to stop treatment." Suppose he applies it in a new arena: There is a time to stop postsurgical treatments, a time to stop reducing the chance of cancer recurring because the treatment creates so much collateral damage. Again, Porter's faith shapes his medical research. A believer who anticipates the resurrection might choose a better life, at the risk of a shorter life.[4] Thus, if Porter's hospital judges everything by survival rates, it may not be the right environment for his research. Porter needs a hospital that respects patients' choices for more or less postoperative treatment, without playing on a patient's understandable fear of death.[5]

Dr. Porter's research illustrates the twin roots of reform through work. His project began when he detected needless suffering. This *spontaneously* led him to see if he could show more mercy to his neighbors, his patients, through better postoperative

4. Believers make this very choice when they decide, for example, not to insert tubes for hydration when a terminally ill cancer sufferer has begun to die.

5. In fact, medicine doesn't always prefer longer life. When travelers want to see wildlife in the Serengeti, they need shots that carry a slight risk of death to prevent diseases with a larger risk. Healthcare providers give the shots, even though the safest course would be to refuse the inoculation and ban international travel.

care. But since Porter had a leadership position and an inclination to use it, his observations led to *organized* acts—a change in protocols for certain cancer patients. So a spontaneous insight led to organized changes.

The same principles hold in other fields, such as relief work. One couple will spontaneously receive an orphan who appears at their door. Another will ask, "Are there other orphans in the area? What can we do for them?" In fact, a large orphanage in northern India began that way. (This story is continued below.) Mother Teresa's work in India among "the poorest of the poor" followed a similar arc from quasi-spontaneous to organized action. Today her Missionaries of Charity have nearly five thousand sisters serving in over one hundred nations. The interest in cancer survivors, orphans, and the terminally ill arises spontaneously, but spontaneous acts can lead people to create institutions that expand it to a long-term enterprise.

Principle, Passion, Position, Perseverance

To summarize, social reform begins as the fruit or spontaneous result of faith and develops from there. My conversations with reformers lead me to conclude that they share several traits, which I will call a principle, a passion, a position, and perseverance. The *principle* is the big idea of a way to make the world a better place. The principle may touch education, manufacturing, medical care, communication, mercy ministry, or anything else.

Passion is the drive to implement the principle. Passion includes infectious enthusiasm, a sense of urgency, an ability to present a case in ways that win partners. Passion is essential because reformers must take risks, overcome obstacles, and tear doors off their hinges to achieve their goals.

Position is a social location with enough formal or informal authority to be heard and to obtain resources. Position includes the ability to create a gifted team that can communicate and implement a new order. It also includes access to essential economic resources.

Perseverance is necessary because reforms rouse opposition, overt or covert. Reforms are messy and provisional at first. Reformers make decisions on the basis of insufficient information. Missteps are inevitable and reformers can't afford to get discouraged and quit when they occur. Principle, passion, position, and perseverance are essential because large-scale efforts require contagious insight, courage, endurance, and a band of colaborers (Eccl. 4:9–12) if one hopes to establish a new order.

Healthy Expression of the Gospel

To return to orphans, when James 1:26–27 names the three marks of true religion, the second is "to visit orphans and widows in their affliction." The verb, *episkeptomai*, signifies a visit with intent to help. Faithful Christians have always pursued this at individual and social levels. Following James, the church has always had a heart for orphans. The first Christians rescued abandoned infants from Greek and Roman garbage heaps where mothers, thinking they could not care for them, abandoned their babies. This was personal, since individuals and families adopted these infants, and it was social, since it changed the way that age treated infants.

Wherever the church goes, it starts orphanages. Church leaders like John Wesley and Philipp Jakob Spener were noted for starting orphanages, and ordinary disciples can do the same. I once visited an orphanage in India that had nearly a thousand children. It started when a Hindu family left a child at the door of a missionary couple. When word spread that the couple received the child, more poverty-stricken parents left their children there. Orphanages love children individually and organizationally, with schedules and budgets. The same holds for hospitals and schools, which often begin as ad hoc responses to a need and become substantial enterprises.

The heroes of the Reformation were social as well as theological reformers. Calvin, living in the age of the plague, took an active interest in Geneva's hospitals. He also promoted industry, especially publishing, since the Protestant refugees who flooded Geneva needed work.

The separation of faith and social action is a rather recent phenomenon. Around 1900, Walter Rauschenbusch, in the age of old liberalism, split social action from the gospel by dropping the gospel. Later, fundamentalists, with separatist impulses, began to withdraw from society. Neither approach coheres with biblical Christianity.

Galatians 6:10 says, "Therefore, as we have opportunity, let us do good to all people, especially to those who belong to the family of believers" (NIV). Believers begin with the church, yet do good to all. Busy people can hear this as an obligation to solve the world's problems. But again, if we do work hard at our job, we *are already* solving the world's problems. The Lord knows we are finite and cannot solve every problem. But we can engage the problems we see, problems that draw our attention, that lie within reach, problems we are equipped to solve.

Thus, while it is admirable to volunteer to aid the sick and the poor, some have expertise there. Therefore, social workers, politicians, and educators may be especially called to help immigrants, the poor, or the uneducated. A physician with a desire to serve the needy will accomplish more by volunteering at a health clinic than by teaching English to immigrants. He might also massage his schedule so he has more time to care for his patient's souls as well as their bodies (regulations permitting).

To say it another way, the distinction between *personal* and *social* ethics seems sharper in Western Christianity than in Scripture. Consider Leviticus 19. It begins with the command, "You shall be holy, for I the LORD your God am holy" (v. 2). Later, God commands, "You shall love your neighbor as yourself: I am the LORD" (v. 18). Notice that the law grounds both commands in God's nature. Notice too that a series of social commands stands between these two apparently personal commands. Leviticus 19:9–10 regulates work in ways that aid the poor. The law begins,

"You shall not strip your vineyard bare" (v. 10). Harvesters must leave gleanings at the edges of the fields so the poor and the sojourner can gather them. Thus, farm work has a social dimension.[6] Farmers care for the poor by giving them tasks to perform, without necessarily employing them. Leviticus adds, "You shall not oppress your neighbor" (v. 13). How so? Employers must pay hired workers at the end of the day.

Next, Moses forbids sins the powerful commit against the weak: "You shall not curse the deaf or put a stumbling block before the blind, but you shall fear your God: I am the LORD" (Lev. 19:14). The law assumes that the strong are tempted to use their abilities viciously. Israelites must not degrade or dehumanize the weak and disabled. Perhaps some think it amusing to curse the deaf; they never know! Or it may grant a sense of power to move an object so the blind stumble. The blind and deaf suffer disadvantages and therefore depend on the kindness of others. "While these people may not be able to hold offenders accountable, *the Lord* most certainly can and will."[7] The deaf and blind represent all who need special care, and the law often addresses them (Lev. 19:9–10; Deut. 27:18; cf. Deut. 10:18; Ps. 68:5).

Leviticus 19:15–16 shows a broader interest in justice. In courts of law, "you shall not be partial to the poor or defer to the great, but in righteousness shall you judge your neighbor." This prohibits all judicial injustice. The strong may abuse their power, but the weak can try to harm the strong too. Resentment and a victim mentality can lead the crowd to mistreat the great. So Moses prohibits all injustice, even if he accents mistreatment of the weak. Elsewhere he says, "You shall take no bribe, for a bribe blinds the clear-sighted and subverts the cause of those who are in the right" (Ex. 23:8; cf. Deut. 16:19). These commands call for justice at every level.

6. This section generally follows Jay Sklar, *Leviticus*, Tyndale Old Testament Commentaries (Downers Grove, IL: InterVarsity, 2014), 242–47.
   7. Ibid., 246.

Common Grace and Reformation

Efforts at reform normally encounter resistance, and the greater the scope of the reform, the greater that resistance. As a result, reformers need allies and cobelligerents who share moral but not theological convictions. As Ecclesiastes says, "A threefold cord is not quickly broken" (4:12), and God's common grace can allow Christians to add cords. Romans 2:14–15 is essential:

> For when Gentiles, who do not have the law, by nature do what the law requires, they are a law to themselves, even though they do not have the law. They show that the work of the law is written on their hearts, while their conscience also bears witness, and their conflicting thoughts accuse or even excuse them.

God graciously restrains the wicked impulses of everyone, believers and unbelievers, largely by granting everyone a conscience and writing his law on each heart. Because God restrains sin, believers may make common cause with outsiders. Václav Havel, Czech dissident from the 1960s to the 1980s, offers a case in point.

Václav Havel (1936–2011) and a Contagious Idea

Václav Havel was a Czech playwright, essayist, troublemaker, and then, surprisingly, a political leader. As a dissident, Havel wrote plays and essays that protested the Soviet-backed communist regime that suffocated his nation. He persevered through years of intimidation and imprisonment, and he refused to relinquish a vision of human flourishing that shared common ground with Abraham Kuyper. Both men pushed against overweening government authority, with Kuyper opposing imperialists and Havel protesting communists.

Havel presented ideas in ways that captured the imagination of millions of Eastern Europeans who lived behind the Iron Curtain. His essay "The Power of the Powerless," originally written in 1978, invites readers to feel the quiet oppression of a humble shopkeeper and to see another way of life. The shopkeeper is a greengrocer who sells fruits and vegetables in his city. He puts a sign in his window: "Workers of the World Unite." It is a venerable communist slogan, but does he put the sign in the window because he believes it? Not at all. He puts it in the window because it came from headquarters, along with the lettuce, carrots, and onions he sells. He puts the sign in the window "because everyone does it, and because that is the way it has to be."[8] If he refuses, there will be accusations of disloyalty and other trouble. The greengrocer doesn't operate in a market economy. "Trouble" means his fruits and vegetables stop coming. He will lose his shop and go to work in a factory with lower pay. Worse, his children will be laborers, with no prospect of a university education. So he puts up the sign. With it, he confesses, "I will behave in the manner expected of me. . . . I am obedient and therefore have the right to be left alone." The sign means "I am afraid and therefore obey without questions."

No one *says* this. It would be degrading to the shopkeeper, who might even rebel over the affront to his dignity. No one says anything. Everyone pretends to live in harmony. Havel calls this "living within the lie." Havel proposed that people living under Soviet domination should stop pretending that all is well. They should begin to "live within the truth," as if the communist regime didn't exist. Yes, the state controlled all businesses and schools and censored the press. But what if Eastern Europeans lived as if they were free and *did* have rights? Suppose a Canadian travels to Poland and stays with friends there. The law requires that he register with the local police upon arrival. He plans to do so until his hosts tell him, "We don't do that anymore. We don't believe the police need to know who stays with us." If one

---

8. Václav Havel, "The Power of the Powerless," in *The Power of the Powerless*, ed. John Keane (1985; repr., London: Routledge, 2015), 40. Find the pdf online at https://tavaana .org/sites/default/files/The%20Power%20of%20the%20Powerless.pdf.

person refuses to register, he faces danger, but if *no one* registers, the law becomes unenforceable and people gain freedom.

Havel urged people to start groups for music, sports, literature, philosophy, publishing, and work, and to create an independent life, so the state would no longer control everything. He called for acts of quiet resistance to the totalitarian state and labeled it "living within the truth." To live in the truth is to stop acting in ways everyone knows to be false. If the grocer doesn't believe the world's workers have united, he should not put the sign in the window. The grocer *pretends* to believe, so he will be left alone and have a marginally better life, materially speaking. Perhaps the shopkeeper doesn't realize, or doesn't care, but when he puts the "Workers of the World Unite" sign in his window, he not only submits; he also *enforces* the very system that suppresses him by quietly pressuring other shopkeepers to put up the sign too.[9] If one shopkeeper refuses the sign, he loses his shop, but if every shopkeeper refuses, all are safe, because the state can't close every shop.

Surprisingly, Poland, the most Christianized nation in the former Soviet bloc, adopted Havel's proposals first. Poles set up illegal printing presses and organized trade unions, although they were needless in communist theory. The pace of liberation quickened, and by 1989 the communist order collapsed. In another surprise, Havel became prime minister of Czechoslovakia and then its successor state, the Czech Republic.

Havel was no Christian, but the concepts of "living within the truth" and "living within the lie" resemble biblical thought. Jesus tells his disciples, "You are the light of the world" (Matt.

9. The terrible genius of the communist system lay in the way it pressed people to enforce their subservience. One childless couple in East Germany was eager to adopt a child. They conducted interviews, filled out forms, and made payments. Their child's due date came, but at the last moment, something went awry. Officials apologized, "I'm sorry, Mr. and Mrs. Schmidt..." Mrs. Schmidt was devastated, but officials encouraged them to apply again. After the same thing happened two more times, Mr. Schmidt asked an official, "What do I need to do?" He agreed to become a petty informant and their baby arrived shortly.

5:14, 16). Paul agrees: "You are light in the Lord. Walk as children of light" (Eph. 5:8). For that reason, disciples "take no part in the unfruitful works of darkness" (Eph. 5:11). As a result, we "shine as lights in the world, holding fast to the word of life" (Phil. 2:12–16). Similarly, John has "great joy" when his people walk "in the truth" (3 John 3).

In Havel's terms, we live within the lie because we fear the consequences of living the truth. In biblical language, because God is light, we walk in light and not in darkness (1 Thess. 5:4; 1 John 1:5–7). Because faith drives out fear, we *can* resist the majority culture (1 John 4:18). Because it is dangerous to be the first to protest, we should find a committed band that can stand together.

The system easily prevails over a person who takes stands alone. To continue discussing communists, we will shift to the 1930s, and meet a young Russian opera singer whose career is surging. He sings the lead tenor role in notable opera houses in Moscow and other cities. One day, after a performance, an official introduces himself and observes, "Mr. Tischkovsky, your career has been going quite well lately. You're very popular. Naturally, people like to go to parties with you after you sing. Next time you have a party, we would like you to invite Sasha Andropov as a guest." It is understood, but not stated, that Andropov is a KGB informant. The official would *never* ask the singer to inform the authorities if his friends made a joke about Stalin; that would be crude. No, he is invited to join the system, to stay prosperous and live a lie by pretending Andropov is just another opera lover.

When Tischkovsky declines to add the KGB agent to his guest list, he isn't beaten or sent to a gulag, but he is reminded that he has a good career, and that he should be grateful for it. If he is not grateful, his engagements might be canceled. Tischkovsky says he *is* grateful, but he cannot invite Mr. Andropov. Soon he sees his engagements canceled, and his family descends into poverty.

I know this story because Tischkovsky was my grandfather. In one sense his story illustrates the plight of a person who stood alone and was crushed, but the full version reveals that his family escaped because of the steadfast intercession of friends in artistic communities in France and America, as well as unseen bureaucrats in the State Department. Truly, "A threefold cord is not quickly broken" (Eccl. 4:12).

Totalitarian states crush lone protesters and free societies ignore or discredit protesters, reformers, and innovators. In principle, for example, advances in efficiency and productivity are welcome since they improve quality or profitability. But theory doesn't always prove itself, since there are ways to sideline or discredit economic competitors.[10] This applies even more in nonprofit sectors, for government, education, and medicine resist reform too.

Conclusion

This chapter has argued that reformations of work are ordinarily the spontaneous result of faith. At best, when God pours his love into our hearts, it fosters compassion for neighbors, whom we love through our work. When circumstances are right, an insight, an invention, or a new system can lead to sizable improvements. If the insight has sponsors who possess passion, position, perseverance, and weighty allies, they may promote systemic change. The next chapter examines how that might happen.

Discussion Questions

1. What does God require of you at work? Has he given you gifts, a cause, a position, or allies that give you a position to effect more reforms? Does he expect more of you?

2. Do you know where you might make your corner of the world a little better? Have you shared this with anyone? Have you begun to pray about it?

---

10. The story of Preston Tucker and his innovative automobiles is a case in point. His company was destroyed, after manufacturing just fifty-one cars, by negative publicity and unfounded allegations of fraud. Many believe large automakers started the rumors because they feared Tucker as a potential competitor.

3. If you have a big idea about a way to change the world, do you have the passion to persevere despite the inevitable opposition? Does opposition scare you?

4. Have you worked with unbelievers on a significant social cause? How did the experience compare to working with fellow believers?

5. Of the quartet—principle, passion, position, and perseverance—which do you have? Which do you lack? Do you have a plan to achieve more?

10

THE THEORY AND PRACTICE OF
REFORMATION THROUGH WORK

The last chapter stressed that reformations at work tend to be spontaneous. It illustrated this with stories about people who work in libraries, orphanages, medical research, and political revolutions. This chapter has two parts: sustained notes on a theory of reform and proposals on the way the theory applies to representative professions (the appendix adds more).

Readers who follow theological debates will see that I endorse Abraham Kuyper's "one kingdom" view of work, not the "two kingdom" view, normally traced to Martin Luther. Advocates of each position are subtle. Subgroups exist, and each side seeks, naturally, to incorporate the best insights of the other. Therefore, I need to simplify the debate, while striving to avoid caricature.[1] Kuyper proposed that Christ is Lord of all of life and that he rules all things (his one kingdom) through his gospel and the comprehensive truth of Scripture. Neo-Kuyperians call the church the vanguard, the concentration point, school, and hospital for disciples, but they don't think Christ's rule of the church is *so very* different from his rule of everything else. Jesus is Lord of every square inch of this world, and he rules all of it in grace, mercy, justice, and faithfulness, as explicated in Scripture.

---

1. In academics, justice is stating opposing views in terms the opponent would approve.

One-kingdom devotees recognize manifest differences between the spheres of life: businesses seek profits and families do not; the church accents grace, the state accents justice. One-kingdom folk see theology as servant of the church, science, and the public. They believe the church *gathers* God's people for worship and instruction and *scatters* them to shine that light on all of life.

Two-kingdom thinkers see it differently. While two-kingdom (or Lutheran) thinkers might affirm most one-kingdom principles, they place their accents elsewhere. W. Bradford Littlejohn says two-kingdom thinkers have

> a desire to re-emphasize the centrality of the Church in the Christian life, a suspicion of over-reaching claims for biblical authority and applicability, a healthy cynicism about the ability to realize gospel norms in temporal and political structures, and a stress on the wide area of commonality between believers and unbelievers in our mundane lives.[2]

Two-kingdom folk agree that God's Word governs all of life, but they believe his rule over politics, economics, science, and technology is "left-handed"—governed by justice and law, not grace. Here *law* is less God's law than natural law. Or it may be *positive law*, the rules of godless kings or legislatures. Positive law may be unfair or exploitive, but believers must follow it and may not think much of changing it, unless it patently contradicts God's Word.[3]

As Littlejohn notes, two-kingdom thinkers suspect that Kuyperians' interest in Christ's lordship over all life, including economics and politics, leads to neglect of the gospel and confusion of faith and works. They also believe it underestimates the

2. W. Bradford Littlejohn, *The Two Kingdoms: A Guide for the Perplexed* (Lincoln, NE: Davenant Trust, 2017), 5.

3. Anabaptists traditionally shun government and military service for the same reason. They believe the military cannot operate on biblical principles. To join it is to be polluted and to attempt to reform them is futile.

common ground or common grace that operates in the public sphere.

This disagreement plays itself out in sundry ways. One-kingdom advocates are more likely to say, with Augustine, that an unjust law is no law. They will ignore it if necessary and change it if possible. Two-kingdom advocates are more likely to urge obedience, since God-ordained authorities promulgated it.

Two-kingdom folk stress common grace in mundane life and sometimes mock one-kingdom rhetoric. At a street level it sounds like this: "Is there a *Christian* way to make a light bulb? To bake a potato? Natural law governs the ways of light and baked potatoes. Whether Christian or pagan, manufacturers and restaurateurs must offer good products and services at fair prices, or they go out of business."

One-kingdom folk reply, "True, there is no Christian potato or light bulb. But faith shapes work globally. Besides serving food, restaurateurs manage people and resources. Are they fatherly toward their staff? Do they try to mitigate the tendency toward alcohol and substance abuse that plagues that industry? Do they close on Sundays to give their people rest? Do they acquire their food and beverages responsibly? If they serve meat, did they ensure that the animals were treated well? Do they follow Proverbs 12:10, 'Whoever is righteous has regard for the life of his beast'?" The same questions apply to light bulbs, throughout the supply chain.

People also question the confidence of neo-Kuyperians. Don't they know that Satan rules this world (John 12:31; 14:30; Rev. 12:9)? Besides, even *believers* can defy God's purposes. Further, sin has noetic effects, so that the mind is as fallen as any other faculty. As a result, efforts to discern God's laws for athletics, engineering, journalism, and medicine will be partial, flawed, and provisional. We will make mistakes and lead people astray. Even when we are right, people will refuse to listen. These observations are valid, and Neo-Kuyperians do not directly dispute them. But they remain hopeful, perhaps even optimistic, about social and economic reform.

Although mankind does suppress God's truth, we remain hopeful, first, because God has written his law on the human heart. Second, although no one can read creation with absolute confidence, God preserved enough order to permit a "pretty good" reading. Third, when we add Scripture and the gift of the Spirit, believers can expect to understand their work reasonably well. Fourth, if one man's will or understanding falters, the community may correct him. So there is reason to hope, to strive for faithfulness, whatever the field. With Scripture in one hand and our (imperfect) reading of creation in the other, we just might be able to reshape our fields of labor. That said, let's consider how we might read creation.

Reading Creation before and after the Fall

In the beginning, God's laws governed all creation, the physical and spiritual alike. Secular scientists puzzle over the presence of physical laws that have held in all places and times since the beginning of time. What is their source? Why do they work so well? They don't seem mysterious to Christians, who believe that God governs through his laws. Thanks to God's faithfulness, humans can discover these laws through observation. That enables humans to fulfill the task God gave us at creation, to develop and protect the earth. When God created mankind, he delegated authority to develop and protect the earth. Humans function as secondary creators and do so through God's norms (Gen. 1:27–30; 2:10–15).[4]

The fall spoiled everything, but Psalms 8, 104, and 147 teach that the creation order still largely holds. Psalm 8 says that God still gives mankind "dominion over the works of [his] hands" (vv. 6–9; cf. Gen. 1–3). Psalm 1, as overture to the Psalter, instructs Israel to meditate on God's Torah—his law or instruction—and so to prosper. All will thrive when humanity, but especially the

---

4. Albert M. Wolters, *Creation Regained: Biblical Basics for a Reformational Worldview*, 2nd ed. (Grand Rapids: Eerdmans, 2009), 21–24. The next several pages are indebted to Wolters.

redeemed, sees that God called mankind to cultivate and guard his creation (Ps. 8:6).

Psalm 104 also celebrates the Lord's good creation. He organized water and land, mountains and valleys (vv. 1–9, 25–26). He ordained the water cycle and the growth of plants, which supports animal life (vv. 10–13, 27). He established darkness, light, and seasons (vv. 19–24). Psalm 147 also praises God's creation. He numbers the stars, sends rain and ice, makes grass grow, and feeds beasts and birds (vv. 4, 8–9, 16–18). He also gives "statutes and rules to Israel" (v. 19). Together, Psalms 8, 104, and 147 announce that God still governs creation so that we can live well in this world.

Theologians like to distinguish the word of God in creation from the word of God in Scripture. But Psalm 147:15–19 says that God's "word runs swiftly" to send ice and frost *and* to declare his "statutes and rules to Israel." That is, the psalm connects the word in creation to the word of redemption. God speaks in both. True, it is harder to hear the word in creation (19:1–3, 7–8). Regardless, Psalms 1, 8, 104, and 147 teach that believers can still discern God's word in creation.[5] That word guides all of life—farming, art, friendship, even humor.

Paul agrees: "Whatever you do, work heartily, as for the Lord and not for men" (Col. 3:23). He says, "So, whether you eat or drink, or whatever you do, do all to the glory of God" (1 Cor. 10:31). Logically, when Paul gives these commands, he implies that we can obey them. First, if Jesus commands his disciples to prove they are his friends by obeying him, they must be *able* to obey. Second, to *obey* God's will, we must *know* it. Third, the command to serve God "whatever you do" implies that *we can discover how to glorify God whatever we do, across the range of human activity*. Thus, comedians, athletes, garbage collectors, and social media mavens alike can read the world *aptly enough* to work faithfully.

5. Ibid., 25–29.

But how? If we exclude God and answer from a secular perspective, there are two answers, both of them incomplete: (1) the good worker obeys the authorities and their rules, or (2) the good worker seeks knowledge, wisdom, skill, and virtue.

If the accent falls on laws and authorities, the good worker follows orders and serves the boss or the tribe. But if laborers simply obey authorities, they abdicate part of their humanity. Obviously, that is repugnant to many, especially if one takes the view that the laws governing society are strictly man-made, without connection to God's law or a universal moral order. This view also gives too much power to the mighty and to the mob.[6] Again, Augustine said an unjust law is no law (*lex iniusta non est lex*). If that is correct, the first view is wrong; it is not enough to obey authorities and rules.

That leads to the second view: A good worker seeks insight, wisdom, skill, and virtue. Aristotle, for instance, believes that intelligent men can interpret the world well enough that, collectively, they can establish a well-functioning society. Unfortunately, many intelligent men, like everyone else, tend to be self-serving. In that vein, Aristotle advocates a slave society where, he claims, slaves cannot govern themselves and so *need* the ruling class to master them. This theory was advantageous for Aristotle and his peers. Today, somewhat similarly, we trust science and technology, since they improve the material conditions of life. Scientists and engineers do bring great benefits, but they gain wealth and prestige too. So we can see that people tend to serve themselves.

This book holds that the mind works best when Scripture guides it. The heart is deceitful and easily rationalizes

---

6. Positive law theory holds that laws are human artifacts that have authority because a properly constituted authority—a legislator, bureaucrat, king, or CEO—declared it. Positive law is apt for the regulation of product labels and traffic, but if applied universally, it denies the existence of an objective moral order. This removes restraints on autocrats and willful majorities. At worst, this view lets dictators like Pol Pot say, "Kill everyone with glasses," and see it done.

self-promoting acts (Jer. 17:9; cf. Prov. 12:5). God's Word reins in selfish tendencies. The command to love our neighbor as ourselves can steer so much of our behavior at work. While writing this chapter, I met a woman who led the design of large office buildings. She loved her work but was buried in its most tedious phase—specifying the tables, chairs, storage spaces, and computer screens that thousands of office workers would use daily. She worked under unconventional rules for office space, in a structure that might stand for a century. It took weeks to do it right, and the lack of creativity frustrated her, since she is a creative type. It helped her to remember that she loved thousands and thousands of people by crafting the best possible work environment for all who would toil in her building. An artisan making chairs could follow the same line, considering how he could love others at every step, from those who supplied his wood to those who bought the chairs.

The Lord did not leave us to guess how to love our neighbors. Jesus adds that his disciples show justice, mercy, and faithfulness (Matt. 23:23). The law also shows us how to love: by honoring authorities, preserving life and property, and telling the truth (Ex. 20).

There is more to say here, and the best way forward is to discuss the theory that is the foundation for application. We will then discuss the practical application for people in leadership.

Wisdom and Creation Ordinances

We begin with a thesis: Leaders must gain experiential wisdom by pursuing love, justice, and faithfulness, all guided by God's law. They may then discern the principles for faithful work in every sphere of life. As we saw earlier in several psalms, God's creation order is substantially intact. As a result, we can find direction for our work by studying creation. Genesis 1–2 describes that order, which operates through a series of foundational institutions. Each has its distinct nature, principles, and authorities. Genesis names work, family, and rest (1:28;

2:1–4, 15, 18–25). Rest provides space for nonproductive activity, as opposed to "total work."[7] Rest also gives space for play, music, artistry, and worship. The growth of family and the development of music and metallurgy lead to education, so the discoveries of one generation reach the next (Gen. 3–4). Education entails the beginnings of science, in the observation of plants, animals, and mankind, as exemplified by Solomon (1 Kings 4:32–34). Next, population growth leads to cities and then to the formation of human economies and governments.

Herman Dooyeweerd proposes that these institutions work best when governed by certain rules. He says that more complex spheres of life build on simpler orders. To simplify, he argues that inanimate matter, existing in space, time, and number, leads to plant and animal life and then to sensation, thought, and emotion. Thought generates communication and education, which occur in families. As humanity develops, skills emerge, which generates more complex economic activity. As economic productivity grows, rest develops into leisure, including play, the arts, sports, and all sorts of specialization and prowess. In this way, human society fosters smaller societies within it, including guilds and the church. The need to coordinate all this invites the development of politics and governance on the practical side and philosophy and ethics on the meditative side.

Structure and Direction

These life-structuring orders are intrinsically good, but they need proper direction; the more potent the structure, the greater its capacity to do good if well-directed and to do harm if not. Certain structures, especially the government and the economy, tend to dominate the others. But each realm has its nature, purpose, and laws, and no aspect of life functions properly when dominated by others.

7. Josef Pieper, *Leisure: The Basis of Culture*, trans. Alexander Dru (Indianapolis: Liberty Fund, 1999), 39–40.

For instance, God ordained government when he told Adam to rule the earth. After the fall, the role of government expanded through population growth. The principal tasks of a nation's government are (1) to ensure the rule of law (Deut. 17:18–20; Prov. 31:4–5; contra 1 Kings 21), (2) to defend its borders from hostile incursions (1 Sam. 17; 2 Sam. 5:17–25; contra 1 Sam. 31), and (3) to protect the weak and the innocent (Prov. 31:5; contra Isa. 5:22–23; 10:1). As a *structure*, therefore, government is good, especially when it fulfills its goals. But the *direction* of government may be good or evil, for some states oppress their own people and seize the land and wealth of neighboring nations.[8]

The military aspect of the state illustrates this. Soldiers have power to kill and therefore seem, at first, to embody evil. But in a fallen world, the military is a necessary instrument of the state, even if it primarily gives diplomats sharp teeth. Because the military can protect peaceful people, believers can consecrate armed forces to God, despite their power to do harm (Luke 3:14; Rom. 13:4). In *structure*, missiles, artillery, and other lethal tools of war project power as instruments of the state, but their *direction* varies. Do rulers order the military to conquer defenseless people? Or do they use the military as a deterrent, to show that a peaceful nation will defend itself and its allies?

When I interviewed a believer who engineers software for the peerless F-15 fighter jet, I asked, "How can you work on machines that are designed to kill?" He replied, "I realize that defensive weapons have offensive capabilities. But my country has enemies, and I see myself as part of its defense." So a fighter jet is good, despite its structure, if, in a war-prone world, political and military leaders use them to keep the peace. In fact, no enemy warplane has shot down an American F-15 for forty years. As a result, no one dares to challenge one in the air, and that has promoted peace.

---

8. Wolters, *Creation Regained*, 59ff.

Sphere Sovereignty

The orders of life function best when they operate according to their principles and stay within their boundaries. Abraham Kuyper (1837–1920) coined the term *sphere sovereignty* to propose that each realm of life has an integrity that includes (1) knowledge of the rules for that sphere, (2) leaders appointed for that sphere, and (3) a resolve to work within its boundaries instead of intruding on other spheres.

Kuyper was ideally positioned to promote sphere sovereignty. His diverse talents led him to work in the church (as a pastor), in communication (by starting several newspapers), in education (by founding a major university), and in politics (by serving as prime minister of the Netherlands). Kuyper observed that each sphere has its norms. As a politician, he detested the absolutist tendency in Europe's monarchies. The state increasingly intruded on all aspects of life, and Kuyper toiled to reverse that by promoting alternative authorities.

Kuyper's followers (neo-Kuyperians) reason that humanity develops through voluntary associations—vocational guilds, churches, and clubs for chess or music.[9] Each association has a charter or essence, and each has its authorities. No association should trample others or be trampled by them. Specifically, the state should not govern (or crush) families, churches, or literary clubs. Credible, competent guild leaders understand the rules of their association and keep outsiders and incompetents from ruining them.

Every association has a purpose and principles that help fulfill it. Car manufacturers, filmmakers, and poetry clubs have their ways. Car makers always have finances in view. Like all businesses, they must create attractive products and sell them profitably, or they die. Literary clubs care about neither sales nor profits. Filmmakers appeal to multitudes; poetry groups do not.

---

9. James Bratt, *Abraham Kuyper: Modern Calvinist, Christian Democrat* (Grand Rapids: Eerdmans, 2013), 133–34.

Since each sphere of life has expert leaders, those leaders should not relinquish their authority to another sphere. And yet, the spheres are not wholly autonomous; they intersect with one another. So the state, whose charter includes protection of its citizens, has a right to order hiking clubs to stop roaming near the borders of hostile neighbors. It also has a right to order filmmakers not to endanger stuntmen. Likewise, parents can challenge education experts if they believe classroom instruction contains misinformation or uses methods that damage their children. Many of our conflicts at work arise when two spheres seem to clash. Suppose a piano teacher has several students who refuse to practice. Should she think, "I'm a musician, not a babysitter," and drop them? Or should she think, "This is my job and if the parents are willing to pay me . . ."?

The concept of sphere sovereignty helped explain the difficulty of reform in the workplace: powerful spheres tended to control weaker ones. So communist states tried to bend everything to state purposes. Newspapers, music, cinema, and literature all had to promote the communist state, which controlled and censored them. Communists believed that promoting the state was more important than telling the truth, so the media pumped out propaganda with enough truth to move the populace to believe strategic falsehoods. Communists also controlled economic enterprise through state planning. Loyalists obtained elite jobs, regardless of merit, while the disloyal languished, even if skilled. Naturally, the economy suffered. The state also intruded on families when the secret police enticed family members to spy on one another.

Today the economy is more likely to exercise dominance. Under communism, the arts submitted to the state; today the arts bend to commerce. If shallow or degrading entertainment sells, it *will* be produced. Markets also commercialize leisure by defining it economically. Thus, dining out or watching a movie counts, but going for a walk barely registers, since it can't be quantified financially.

Economic forces have also transformed sports recently, not necessarily for the better. Professional sports generate billions of dollars,[10] but we also commercialize children's sports through leagues, traveling teams, and expensive coaches. Perversely, universities commonly recruit athletic stars more avidly than intellectual stars because athletic programs generate more income (and top college coaches earn vastly more than college presidents). Intense training and competition lead to traumatic injuries, especially the damage caused by repeated blows to the head in soccer, football, boxing, and hockey.[11] Our culture says that if athletes suffer brain or ligament and tendon damage, well, they should have known the risks. Most coaches love their players and earnestly seek their good, but economic factors can impel coaches to win—or else. Competitive fire in players and an interest in job security can push key players to get back in the game before they are ready, at the cost of lifelong injury.

The marketplace can hurt health care too. Efforts to control medical costs limit most appointments to fifteen minutes, so physicians lack time for the deep listening that allows accurate diagnosis (see appendix). If physicians become "health-care providers" who have "clients," rather than patients, the doctor-patient bond is reduced to an economic transaction. The drive to control costs can even prevent necessary therapy, while the for-profit side of medicine can promote treatments that increase revenue but hardly serve patients.

Churches feel economic pressures too. The consumer

10. Recent statistics report these annual incomes for leading professional leagues, worldwide: soccer: $40 billion; baseball: $13 billion; NFL football: $13 billion; basketball: $10 billion.

11. The data are complex. The most lethal high school sport is baseball/softball; football ranks fourth. Cheerleading causes the most injuries, but football, followed closely by hockey and soccer, causes the most concussions. Ninety-nine percent of professional football players whose brains have been posthumously examined suffered chronic traumatic encephalopathy (CTE). But it is possible that changes to the game, including concussion protocols, have reduced the damage. Beyond that, all exercise entails a degree of risk, and a complete failure to exercise probably brings an even greater risk.

mentality lets Westerners view the church as a provider of spiritual services. If it fails to deliver a good product, then they say so and switch vendors. Consumers think about church contractually. Church is a place to obtain benefits rather than a community bound by a covenant with God and one another. Pastors hear that the church should operate more like a business, but the church is the antithesis of a business. Like Jesus, it gives away its services. That said, the church does have an economic aspect because it has employees and meeting spaces. If it pays no heed to financial realities, its mission will suffer—and that holds for any organized activity.

To summarize, each sphere of life has its expertise. Each needs to keep others from intruding, yet each needs to learn from the others, since every aspect of life is connected. Consider the case of David Dao, who had settled in his airline seat to fly from Chicago to Louisville when flight attendants ordered him to leave the plane to make room for late arriving airline personnel. When Dao refused, security dragged him from the plane so violently that he suffered a concussion and a broken nose. Violence aside, the incident aligned with airline policies, which assert a right to overbook flights and then remove ticketed, seated passengers, should too many arrive. In their system, overbooking is *rational*, since it maximizes profits by minimizing empty seats. But is it right? Renowned economist Milton Friedman would argue that the policy makes sense, since "there is one and only one social responsibility of business—to use its resources and engage in activities designed to increase its profits so long as it stays within the rules of the game, which is to say, engages in open and free competition without deception or fraud."[12]

Friedman's view prevails in most of America's corporations. Financial calculations drive airline decisions. But what if the

---

12. Milton Friedman, *Capitalism and Freedom* (Chicago: University of Chicago Press, 1962), 133. Friedman also wrote for the public; see Milton Friedman, "The Social Responsibility of Business Is to Increase Its Profits," *New York Times Magazine*, September 13, 1970.

displaced passenger is the keynote speaker at a conference? What if someone misses a family wedding? Airlines should allow the needs of their customers in the *social* sphere to temper their profit motives in the economic sphere, since people often fly for social reasons. Since faithfulness is essential to social bonds, respect for customers should shape airline policy too. Predictably, certain airlines have found that treating customers well is good for business. The state could also decide that mistreatment of passengers is a legal matter.[13]

But let's turn to a happier case, one that shows how a principle, joined with passion, position, and partners, can reform work. It also describes a spontaneous insight that gained a permanent institutional life.

Adam Ross, CEO of Brick Corps[14]

A business makes a profit or it dies, and yet, I propose, the ideal business is motivated by love, justice, and faithfulness, not just by profits.

Adam Ross is the CEO of Brick Corps, a rapidly growing construction firm with annual sales of seven billion dollars. Ross, rather improbably, left the construction industry for two years to obtain a seminary degree, then returned to a place where his faith manifests itself in his desire to construct good buildings while reducing costs, increasing profits, and treating people well.

Construction is a cyclical business, with booms and busts, and a year can be lean or prosperous, apart from industry trends. This requires firms to stay nimble and develop sound personnel policies. Those policies help employees like Michelle Strong, a single, award-winning architect, thrive at Brick Corps. Michelle's story puts the policies at Brick Corps into perspective.

Shortly after she finished college, Michelle joined BJX, a prestigious firm where she worked on several yearlong projects,

---

13. Space permitting, one might consider how finance corrupts politics, schools, and churches.

14. I have changed names and details in this story because of a desire for anonymity.

including an airport and a stadium. The week she finished the stadium, a supervisor called her in, thanked her, and told her to pack up her desk.[15] Michelle had strong reviews and everyone liked her, but BJX cut her because they controlled costs (maximized profits) through constant layoffs. Michelle knew BJX did this. Everyone knew it; in fact, firms that needed architects tracked BJX layoffs. Brick Corps quickly hired Michelle. Although construction is a male-dominated field, Brick Corps respects capable women, and Michelle became a vice president by the age of forty.

Just as important, Brick Corps has a distinct approach to employment. Adam Ross explains, "We don't lay off good people. We don't believe that's the way to build a company. Besides, money isn't necessarily the most important thing for us." In fact, Brick Corps is highly profitable, and treating people well is vital to its success. Its offices are ergonomically sound, and its gathering spaces are attractive. They have a well-equipped gym with a personal trainer, so their employees can stay fit. Additional amenities simplify life for their staff. These policies help retain talented people, but that isn't the way Ross explains himself:

> Layoffs are one way to do business, but it's not the way we operate. We take care of people, but not because we hope somebody admires us. We don't do it for the effects or the bottom line. We do it because we know who we are, what kind of business we're designed to be.

Brick Corps believes that people are its chief resource, and it tries, however imperfectly, to live that out. They believe that if they lose good people, performance suffers. None of this means Brick Corps is soft on its staff. Far from it. Each year, they rank all employees to identify who is thriving and who is languishing. They cull the bottom ranks, both to protect their business and

---

15. We could see this as BJX taking a half step toward the gig economy (see chap. 1).

to let faltering employees find work that better matches their skills. Strikingly, during one down cycle, they did not cut one qualified worker. Instead, everyone took a 10 percent pay cut. That dedication also showed in one of Michelle's reviews. Her boss told her she had to work fewer hours. "We can't let you burn out." So Michelle plans to stay at Brick Corps, whatever job offers come her way. It's easy to stay at a place that treats its employees with dignity.[16]

Ross sees the flaws at Brick Corps. As a Christian, he has a robust sense of his need for grace. He knows that his sins and flaws affect his work. To change his company, he has to change himself and that, he confesses, "is a messy proposition." He quotes Peter Kreeft, "This world is a vale of soul-making, a great sculptor's shop and we are his statues. To be finished, the statues must endure many blows of the chisel. . . . This is not optional." Once we have lost our innocence, the way back to God must be hard.[17]

As a believer, Ross wants to be faithful as well as successful. But he doesn't emphasize rules and rejects the quest for perfection. "I want my people to see my struggle, not an illusion of control or moral perfection. Then they can trust me." Then, he believes, they can change the world of design and construction. His plans include vertical integration of the construction process, drone-based contour mapping, and large-scale 3-D printing, but that is another story.

This is the kind of reform our age needs, one that joins technical expertise and humanity. We need reformers with the passion to fight for their proposals, from a position that lets them implement their ideas. The best reformers also have the will to persevere through inevitable resistance. Like Porter (chap. 9), Ross believes that the best innovations proceed from both professional and biblical insights. Porter believes that God created the body with powers of recovery that physicians should not impede.

16. BJX tried to rehire Michelle shortly after she won an award. But why would she leave her company for one that dumps people to save a few dollars?

17. Peter Kreeft, *Three Philosophies of Life* (San Francisco: Ignatius Press, 1989), 85.

He also believes survival rates should not be the sole criteria of medical success. Ross wants to put up great buildings, profitably, while treating people well, even if profits dip in the short run.

Thus, in a market economy, businesses must be profitable, but profit must not be the sole criterion for success. Further, the quality of life degenerates when the state or the economy trumps all and reduces family, religion, and the arts to aspects of politics and economics.

Conditions for Reform

With these principles in hand, we can name preconditions or frameworks for social reform through work. First, leaders must master the norms that govern their field. Second, competent authorities must promote or defend those norms. Third, authorities in diverse fields must heed one another where their activities overlap. The principles for reform are these:

1. Love, justice, and faithfulness, as explicated in Scripture, must guide every endeavor.
2. Led by those values, leaders fallibly apply the norms of their discipline or occupation to areas under their authority, especially where there is deformity or inequity, and when the essentials of God's Word and their field are ignored.
3. Leaders identify economic, political, social, or philosophical barriers to reform, and they do not forget the weight of inertia and fear of change.
4. Reformers identify areas where reform is feasible, where conditions are more likely to let plans succeed. This includes the ability to gain capable allies, whatever their faith or convictions.

Discovering the Rules

Earlier in this chapter, I proposed that *experiential wisdom, combined with love, justice, and faithfulness, should allow leaders to discern the primary principles for faithful action in every sphere of life.*[18] Two short case studies will show how love, justice, and faithfulness, informed by the Ten Commandments, guide athletics, but leave us with substantial questions regarding food production.

We begin with *amateur sports.* Since I have played and occasionally coached competitive sports (especially tennis) throughout my life, I hope I have gained a modicum of wisdom. In competitive athletics, justice requires players to know and adhere to the rules of the game—without cheating! A major joy of sport lies in the way competition brings out the best in athletes. Therefore, we strive to win, but not at all costs. Love teaches athletes to avoid dangerous play and to respect their opponents. The preamble to the rules for ultimate frisbee states the ideal: "Ultimate relies upon a Spirit of the Game that places the responsibility for fair play on every player. . . . *Highly competitive play is encouraged, but should never sacrifice the mutual respect between players, adherence to the agreed-upon rules of the game, or the basic joy of play.*"[19] Faithfulness also directs organizers to arrange competitions in ways that give many a chance to win. Athletes learn to play hard, even when weary, if only for the sake of their teammates. The law forbids that athletes aim to wound their opponents, since "you shall not kill" covers lesser injuries. Since the *ideal* outcome for boxing is to beat an opponent into unconsciousness, it seems immoral. This raises questions about sports that cause brain damage. While we recognize efforts to reduce brain injuries in football, for example, the principle of caution should make parents pause before sending their sons onto that field.

Let's switch to food production. Justice and love guide food workers to provide the daily bread that sustains life. In times of abundance, they help people celebrate life with delicious food and drink, for they gladden the heart (Deut. 14:26; Ps. 104:15; Song 7:13; John 2:1–12). Festive meals promote conviviality and

---

18. Perhaps "experiential wisdom" resembles what Catholic writers call natural law.
19. "What Is Spirit?," World Flying Disc Federation, http://www.wfdf.org/sotg/about-sotg.

pleasures for the eye and the palate. And we always hope that food will be sufficient, clean, and nutritious. But there are intense debates about food. In the past, mankind struggled to generate enough food. Most people produced food by growing crops or tending animals. But rapid gains in productivity since 1900 have created an abundance of food. Today, in many places, obesity is a bigger problem than scarcity. The time spent alleviating hunger dwindles, and conversations on the processing, packaging, and marketing of food increase. How shall the nutritional value of processed foods be labeled? Is it honest to call a block of sugar an "energy bar"? Critics argue that the snack food industry calibrates the levels of salt, fat, sugar, and fiber to promote overeating. Because candy and chips lack fiber, people don't feel sated and keep munching. And yet in other parts of the world, many still starve. What do prosperous nations owe them? Food shipments? Better seeds? Training in land management? Respect for the land is part of biblical law. Indeed, Scripture links land management and care for the poor, since lack of land connects to a lack of food.[20]

Food preparers have debates too. What is the best practice for quick meals? Can we agree on the traits of healthy cooking and eating? Salt and butter taste good, but in excess they cause harm. Should chefs guard the health of their patrons or give them what they want and keep tables full? Does that question show that economics is intruding, or is it mere realism: restaurants need happy customers?

Evaluating these ideas for athletics and food preparation, we notice that each field features agreement and conflict. The areas of consensus might provoke overconfidence, while the disagreements could spawn despair. Instead, let us say that God, in his common grace, restrains sin (Gen. 11:6–9) and offers temporal blessings to all (Matt. 5:45). Therefore, even capable unbelievers

20. Christopher J. H. Wright, *Old Testament Ethics for the People of God* (Downers Grove, IL: InterVarsity, 2004), 76–97.

can discern substantial truth and practice the good (Luke 6:33; Rom. 2:14–15).[21]

According to Isaiah 28:23–29, God instructs farmers so they know how to raise good crops in their time and place:

> Give attention, and hear my speech.
> Does he who plows for sowing plow continually?
>   Does he continually open and harrow his ground?
> When he has leveled its surface,
>   does he not scatter dill, sow cumin,
> and put in wheat in rows
>   and barley in its proper place,
>   and emmer as the border?
> For he is rightly instructed;
>   his God teaches him.
>
> Dill is not threshed with a threshing sledge,
>   nor is a cart wheel rolled over cumin,
> but dill is beaten out with a stick,
>   and cumin with a rod.
> Does one crush grain for bread?
>   No, he does not thresh it forever. . . .
> This also comes from the LORD of hosts;
>   he is wonderful in counsel
>   and excellent in wisdom.

A skeptic might contend that it is beneath God's dignity to instruct farmers in the methods of Middle Eastern, Iron Age agriculture. But no—if God cares for mankind, he cares that we eat. Therefore, he instructs farmers. This instruction came, we suppose, not by direct divine speech, but through the collective insight of skilled farmers.

---

21. John Frame, *Systematic Theology: An Introduction to Christian Belief* (Phillipsburg, NJ: P&R Publishing, 2013), 246–48.

More broadly, Isaiah says God teaches mankind how to work both through Scripture and through men and women who excel at their craft. In Proverbs, one gains wisdom by heeding instruction and by watching how the world works. What happens when a farmer sleeps at harvest? Hunger looms. When one entrusts a message to a fool? Confusion reigns. When a ruler drinks to excess? Injustice prevails. "It is not for kings to drink wine, or for rulers to take strong drink, lest they . . . forget what has been decreed and pervert the rights of all the afflicted" (Prov. 31:4–5).

Scripture and wisdom are accessible, yet work is complicated enough that we expect errors and stay open to correction.[22] We will not return to Eden, but we strive to restore parts of this fractured world through the arts of physical and spiritual healing. We also develop the natural world. As historical creatures, we expect this to unfold over time as we learn from both geniuses and fools. We also expect each culture, in its place and time, to develop in distinct ways and so to add to human achievement (Acts 17:26–27).

The world does not yield its secrets easily. Since the fall, weeds and bugs, whether six-legged or electronic, disrupt work. Locusts, droughts, wars, sloth, criminality, and fecklessness conspire to hide God's design and make plans difficult to execute. Still, God did not abandon this world and neither should we.

So it is possible to "work heartily" for the Lord, in all ethical, life-giving occupations. God's creation is good, and it is wrong to require abstinence from it, for "everything created by God is good, and nothing is to be rejected if it is received with thanksgiving, for it is made holy by the word of God and prayer" (1 Tim. 4:4–5).

Seeing Every Field as Sacred

If all creation is good, when consecrated by the Word, there is no place for a sacred-secular split. So we should not call journalism a "secular guild." Rather, godless journalism is secular,

22. Wolters, *Creation Regained*, 32–42.

but journalism is sacred when it follows God's ideals for communication: speak the truth in love and try to edify (Eph. 4:15–29). In the arts, we do not claim a sculpture of Jesus is sacred and a sculpture of a servant is secular. All art can be sacred. For Michelangelo, *The Pietà* is sacred because of the subject matter. But Vermeer's milkmaid is sacred because he respects her and her labor, and he adorns her with light and color.

Likewise, we do not say that a chef does sacred work when he volunteers in a soup kitchen, but secular work when he labors in his restaurant. All cooking is sacred if joy infuses the food and it nourishes people. We do not say accountants do sacred work when they examine the books of a mercy ministry, but secular work when they serve software companies. Architects and builders can do sacred work whether they design churches, hospitals, or apartments. It is sacred to create spaces that let people flourish, when the form enhances the function of the space, and there is all the beauty that the budget allows.[23] All honest work is sacred when devoted to the glory of God.

Work is sacred if it follows God's law, if the motive is love for neighbor. It is sacred if it reverses godless and immoral practices that have crept into its guild, if it battles the systemic evils that shape the work.

Challenging Cases of Reform at Work

But how might we resist systemic evils? Earlier we proposed that believers strive for reforms when essential rules for a field are widely ignored. But what if evils are entrenched and biblical wisdom enjoys little support? What if great powers stymie all efforts at reform? With food, the profit motive may thwart efforts to promote healthy eating. In sports, football's commercial power may impede efforts to protect players. No one wants to blow

---

23. To deny the *sacred-secular split* is also to affirm the priesthood of believers. Peter said, "You are . . . a royal priesthood" (1 Peter 2:9). That indicates that every believer—not just clerics—can do dignified work that serves humanity and does what God asks and desires.

up the gold mine. Sensible reformers will identify the common ground that they share with potential allies, whatever their faith commitments. *All* parents of children who love football have the standing to press for safety.

Reform as Radical, Not Revolutionary

The goal is reform that is *radical, not revolutionary.* Biblical reform is not violent; it goes to the root cause (Latin: *radix* = radical), believing that steady effort may eventually bring lasting change. That is how Paul overthrew slavery. He never says, "Death to slavery." But when he sends a runaway slave, Onesimus, back to his owner, Philemon, his cover letter (the Epistle to Philemon) undermines the basis for slavery. Paul gently urges Philemon to liberate Onesimus. He tells both men they are brothers (Philem. 1:15–17). If they are brothers, how can one enslave the other?

If we seek reform that is radical, not revolutionary, we must work with existing leaders. Sixteenth-century Protestants had a debate. When facing persecution at the hand of Catholics, what should Protestants do? Flee? Yes, if possible. Deny their faith? No, although they could hide. Resist forcefully? Most said no, but when violent Catholic monarchs executed thousands of their own Protestant citizens, debates about self-defense quickened. Luther never advocated military resistance, but Calvin vacillated. He urged private citizens to obey "arrogant kings," but he eventually said "the lesser magistrate" has a duty "to withstand kings who . . . violently assault" their own people. Indeed if they "wink at" such violence, they are guilty of "nefarious perfidy."[24] The concept of resistance by a "lesser magistrate" allows orderly change because it respects existing authorities. That is also the way forward today. By appealing to the best elements of their culture and to leaders with a sense of justice, reformers can locate the allies they need.

---

24. John Calvin, *Institutes of the Christian Religion,* trans. Ford Lewis Battles (Philadelphia: Westminster Press, 1961), 4.20.31 (1518–19); Bruce Gordon, *Calvin* (New Haven, CT: Yale University Press, 2009), 320–28.

Conclusion

This chapter, this book, has argued that we can hope to effect life-giving social reforms through work. The principles of love, justice, and faithfulness, joined to God's grace and law, offer direction. Substantial order remains in creation, so that the wise, taught by God, can see a way forward. Further, God preserves the structures that govern his world, even after the fall. Each structure or realm has its sphere of competence, its rules, and its wisdom. Sin corrupts every sphere, and the great powers, especially commerce and government, habitually abuse their authority. The quest for wealth tries to mandate that certain things *must* be done, and the powerful defend their status and the status quo, so that every effort at reform is precarious. Yet each culture retains points of contact with God's truth, so we can proceed with hope.

This book maintains that despite human sin, the cultural mandate (that is, God's charge to the first humans to govern and develop the earth) still stands. We dare to think Christians can do more than make a living or avoid sin. We show that Christ, the King, has come and that his kingdom has arrived, even in our work, in every realm of life.

Some scoff at this. They deny that there is a "Christian" way to make T-shirts or chicken sandwiches or "Christian" math or history. Fair enough, but the words on a T-shirt can please God or grieve him, and there are right and wrong ways to treat chickens and food workers. And even if math and history are objective, one must still decide which math problems to solve and which past events merit investigation. Faith commitments shape those decisions.

We recognize satisfied workers when we see them. A librarian places books into the hands of students, and when returning the book, they ask, "Did he write anything else?" The physician watches a patient stride into the office, beaming, a month after a near-death experience. Parents hear their child sing her first lullaby. Should we think these are the fortunate few whose skills match their setting? Not necessarily. Perhaps we can make these joys more common as we reform both sides of work: our subjective attitudes and its objective conditions.

I close with an exhortation. Efforts at reform start with individuals. Ideally, they find a group, with partners and mentors. Reformers see how sin affects us all and bring light and justice to their age. In business, they say *no* to economically advantageous sins. Employers refuse to treat workers as mere production costs, and employees resist the temptation to extract everything possible from employers. We do not make or market products we know to be harmful. We promote human flourishing by offering food, shelter, education, and health. All of this is easier said than done. Knowing that, believers turn to God both for the grace that empowers our labors and for the grace that forgives our failures, trusting that both flow from the Lord Jesus, carpenter and redeemer, the supreme worker who "loved us and gave himself up for us" (Eph. 5:2) and invites us to follow him.

Discussion Questions

1. Do you believe Jesus is Lord of every square inch of life (the one-kingdom view)? How does that shape your life in work, politics, or elsewhere?

2. Do you agree that a disciple can work for the military? For a company that designs or manufactures weapons? Why or why not?

3. Have you seen any area where God may be calling you to restructure your part of the world? Please describe it. Do you have an action plan? A prayer pattern?

4. Explain these concepts: common grace, structure and direction, sphere sovereignty, and radical not revolutionary. How do these ideas shape our work, paid or unpaid?

5. Share your reaction to any of the stories in the last two chapters: Clay Porter's new way to treat cancer patients, the political work of Václav Havel, the "we don't discard good people" stance of Mark Ross, or the expulsion of

David Dao from a plane. What lessons do these stories convey?

6. Where has God's common grace enabled you to make common cause with an unbeliever with whom you shared a goal? What did you learn from the experience?

7. Have you seen economics or politics overwhelm other aspects of life? What happened? Can you protect the integrity of any aspect of creation from violation of sovereignty in its sphere?

8. If you shared one thought from this book with your best friend, what would it be?

APPENDIX

PRINCIPLES FOR
REPRESENTATIVE PROFESSIONS

As I interviewed people for this book, Emma, the founder of a growing design firm, pressed me to offer more than general principles for work: "I need you to tell me what to do on Mondays. What I do if someone remarks about 'incentives'—bribes or kickbacks—that would make him more favorable toward a bid. And is it moral for me to fire people who need their job but aren't performing? Also, I know the Bible prohibits interest, but my entire industry runs on loans. How can I finance projects without loans? I need help with *specifics*."

This appendix attempts to heed Emma's call. I can answer her questions: First, because the Bible forbids bribery (Ex. 23:8; Deut. 16:19; Prov. 17:23) and financial deceit (Deut. 25:13; Prov. 20:10), Emma will need to decide how to decline requests for "incentives." A mix of selective deafness and *legal* perks may be best. People can treat business partners to dinners, concerts, and athletic events because the bonds that form there have a legitimate business purpose. Second, as chapter 3 explained, a dismissal can be an act of love and justice, both for the faltering individual and for teams that suffer when one member cannot carry his or her load. Third, the Bible forbids interest on loans to the *poor* (Ex. 22:25), but it doesn't forbid all interest. In fact, in both the parable of the talents and the parable of the minas, Jesus assumes that it is legitimate to earn interest when loaning money for business (Matt. 25:27; Luke 19:23). The rules for loans to the poor and loans for business are different. For the first, interest is forbidden; for the second, it is normal. That said, Emma also has many questions that theologians and pastors cannot answer. Since we know little about design, we have left our sphere of competence and ought to be silent. When pastors meet with groups of professionals in medicine, business, engineering, or media, the format should be neither lecture nor ordinary dialogue. Either the pastor or the professionals can set the agenda. If the professionals lead, they might say, "We believe the Bible sheds light on our work through teachings a, b, c, and d. Have we understood it correctly? What can you add? Also, as we practice our craft, we encounter ethical problems a, b, and c. Can you offer us guidance?" Ideally, the pastor may comment briefly, leading to a wide-ranging discussion during which the pastor may essentially be a listener.

If a pastor or theologian convenes a gathering, he might begin, "I have tried to learn certain essentials about your field and have heard you describe your challenges. While I have no expertise in your discipline, I can mention biblical principles that relate to your tasks." When the pastor finishes, he cedes leadership of the discussion to others. He listens and comments as invited.

When writing, the author essentially convenes groups of readers who will, he hopes, discuss, assess, and apply his proposals. Sadly, I cannot hear your feedback, so I can only promise that I have discussed my proposals with people in each field. In that spirit, I humbly propose applications of biblical principles for eight occupations: coaches and tutors, communicators, entertainers, health-care providers, soldiers, managers, educators, and builders and manufacturers.

I offer five resolutions, or principles, for disciples at work. They begin with "we," not "I," because work is communal. "We" asserts that work has public and social dimensions, even if one works in isolation. Even if one makes cellos alone in a shop, the cellos affect men and women who will play and hear them years later and miles away. Here are the five principles:

1. We will strive for godlike justice, faithfulness, and love. Love includes a generous spirit and mercy toward failure.
2. We will apply God's law, especially the Ten Commandments, to all work.
3. We will promote worthy causes and goals.
4. We will look for people we can serve, develop, and protect.
5. We will follow the examples of heroes at work. We are always apprentices, learning to practice the faith by following experts.[1]

With these principles in hand, we delve into particular fields. For the first two fields, I will note places where the principles apply, to help readers see how they manifest themselves.

Coaches, Private Teachers, and Tutors

I begin with coaches and tutors since most readers will have experience with one. Millions of people coach sports or fitness groups, teach music or the arts, or tutor students. The common thread is intense work with small groups or individuals who are seeking personal development. Coaches and tutors readily show love, justice, and faithfulness in private instruction (1). *Justice* requires instructors to sufficiently master their field to convey the basics to beginners and complex skills to advanced students. Tutors set achievable yet challenging goals for their students (3), and when they can no longer help them, they admit it and defer to the next instructor (4).

In sports, fair play and good sportsmanship obey the laws requiring honesty and love. But love also includes joy in the game and in one's teammates, as well as respect for rivals. Godly

---

1. Kevin J. Vanhoozer, *Faith Speaking Understanding: Performing the Drama of Doctrine* (Louisville, KY: Westminster John Knox, 2014), 7.

athletes are gracious in victory and defeat. Love for the community also applies to individual activities like painting or running since everyone can encourage and exchange helpful information with a neighbor.

Faithful coaches present methods for improvement, including principles for effective practice. Tutors don't let their people quit; the heroes of the faith didn't (5). The goal is not to practice until "I can do it right," but to practice until I can hardly do it wrong, even under pressure. By enduring, musicians and athletes bring out the best in themselves. Coaches and teachers also foster teamwork. Musicians sing or play together as voices and instruments blend; individual athletes work as a team to win games. In both systems, leaders let talented players soar *and* keep teams intact.

Good instructors have a plan for everyone, whether they have great talent or not. They watch their speech. When students or players fail, godly coaches never insult or demean them, since that wounds the spirit (4). But they also shun the false praise and flattery that keep clients taking lessons. Instead, they offer gentle but honest critique and accurate praise.

Communicators

Let's remember our basic principles, in brief form:

1. We seek justice, faithfulness, and love.
2. We apply God's law to our work.
3. We promote worthy causes and goals.
4. We look for people to serve, develop, and protect.
5. We follow the examples of heroes at work.

News people show justice (1) by reporting accurately and treating sources responsibly. They refuse to publish groundless accusations. They weigh the damage a *true* report can cause to innocent people (4, commandments 8 and 9). They prefer to report on worthy causes, not trivia. They turn eyes and ears in the right direction. They love others by telling the truth in ways that help the people *to whom* they communicate and respect the people *about whom* they communicate. They know that speech can be vain or pointless, not just false. The ninth commandment—"You shall not bear false witness" (Ex. 20:16)—reveals that false reports can cause legal harm. When they damage a reputation, they impair the ability to work.

Journalists and corporate writers promote *accurate* speech. God is the model (5), for he is the God of truth and his gospel is "the word of truth" (2 Tim. 2:15; see also Isa. 65:16; John 14:6; 17:17; Eph. 1:13). The best interviewers elicit proper self-revelation. They detect the essence of a story and see through self-justifying, self-promoting nonsense. They call out false claims or ludicrous promises. At worst, the media trade in half-truths, rumors, and exaggerations. Both gossip (taking the truth where it should not go) and slander (presenting fabrications as facts) appear in the Bible's vice lists. Both tempt the media because they can spike ratings (Rom. 1:29–30; 16:18).

Honest communication tells the truth *helpfully*. Writers and broadcasters tell the truth *beautifully* by giving it the right setting, so that it informs, persuades, delights, and invites contemplation (Prov. 25:11–12; Eph. 4:15; Col. 3). Humor, irony, and wordplay are the hand–whipped cream on the raspberry torte.

The basic principles for writers seem obvious: no plagiarism or falsehoods, unless writing fiction or comedy. They should write, as Calvin said, with clarity, brevity, and wit. They must also examine their goals and motives. If to entertain, they aim to delight their readers. If to educate or persuade, they invite reflection. Ideally, authors challenge their audiences. But the craft of writing spurs debates. Should writers tell it "straight," spelling everything out, or tell it "slant," as Jesus did, with stories and nonlinear reasoning? Should we focus on a narrow, core audience or engage outsiders? Are procedures different for critical and controversial writings? Do we handle friendly and hostile (even dangerous) opponents in the same manner? In debates, love and justice dictate that we state an opponent's views in terms they consider accurate. But not everyone agrees. Political writers want to win however they can, and distorting an opponent's record is considered fair play.

At best, the media promote justice, especially for the powerless (3). They shine light on evil deeds, but turn it away from private matters that could bring needless shame. They harm no one, whether by falsehood or carelessness (4). They let confidential matters remain so. Oliver Sipple, a former Marine, saved the life of President Gerald Ford in 1975. Sipple was standing beside an assassin just as she lifted her gun to fire. When he knocked the gun down, the media hailed Sipple as a hero. But when they investigated his personal life, they uncovered personal matters he wished to keep secret. Sipple pleaded for privacy, but the media saw him as a public figure with no right to privacy. They revealed everything, initiating a cascade of events that ended in Sipple's premature death.

Scripture says communicators should "speak the truth in love" and "give grace to those who hear" (Eph. 4:15, 29). "Truth" means real accuracy, not minimal approximations of it (but what are the guideline for programs that are more like food fights than serious conversations?). They overlook minor slips and take inopportune comments in the best sense. Ideally, they convey helpful, even transforming, information (3).

Entertainers

In the film *Stardust Memories*, a group of aliens encounters a comedian who wants to serve humanity, and he asks for their counsel. They reply, "You want to do mankind a *real* service? Tell funnier jokes!" Paul might add, "Funny jokes, but not crude jests or mockery of sacred things" (see Eph. 4:29). It is good to laugh at silliness, like the quirks of human language and customs. When Solomon mocks the sluggard, who sleeps all morning because there could be a lion in the street, he shows that it's good to laugh at folly (Prov. 26:13–15).

There is no rule book for comedy (or drama). Till then, the princes of comedy and drama try to figure out an ethic for entertainment: Is it right to curse or show violence to represent the human condition properly? How might we depict wickedness accurately, even empathetically, without making villainy entrancing? Can we make heroes more interesting than villains? How can we promote virtue without getting didactic? How can entertainment help us forget our sorrows (Prov. 31:7)? How can we laugh with each other, but not at each other? How do we entertain without pandering to customers or becoming self-indulgent? Can we "make 'em laugh" and "give them what they want" while also *elevating* what they want?

Let's consider a difficult case, the exploitation of women in entertainment. In 2017–18, the long-simmering, long-suppressed scandal of the sexual harassment of female actors broke containment. It began when several strong entertainers credibly accused the worst offenders of sexual harassment. Suddenly, renowned men faced charges for pressing (even forcing) women to provide sexual favors and threatening reprisals if they refused or spoke up afterward. Once a few women came forward, the floodgates opened. The tide began with entertainers and was followed by women in business, the media, and hospitality. Most charges were credible, and titans of entertainment, business, and politics resigned in disgrace.

Will this change the lives of women? Reform is difficult because people tend to persist in established patterns. Change may be especially difficult in cinema because sex sells. We must ask if society is willing to see a connection between the way fictional worlds objectify women and the way the real world does. One mogul (Harvey Weinstein) produced an array of award-winning films but was banned from the film industry for pressing actresses to perform sexual acts in *private*. Ironically, a number of his *award-winning* films required actresses to undress or perform sexual acts for the *public*. The film industry attracts viewers, in part, by presenting sexual activity, nudity, violence, and depraved acts in ways that millions find entertaining. Are certain men drawn to the *depiction* of sensuality in cinema because they are drawn to it personally? Apparently, some choose not to distinguish fictional performance on screen from the behavior they desire in private.[2] Reform of cinema will be difficult. Sex and violence offer potent vicarious thrills. Yet, as Charles Taylor argues, every culture has "cross-pressures" that counter its dominant values.[3] Here the cross-pressure is the passion for justice and women's rights. But are people willing to see the connection between the objectification of women in films and their objectification in reality? If women are constantly sexualized on screens, should we be shocked if that has an effect off the screen? Indeed, objectification and dehumanization seem to link sexualized films, prostitution, and porn.

Reform might begin in the marketplace, since family-friendly films tend to be more profitable. Parents could teach their children what they need to know about sexuality and respect. If disciples stopped watching sexually immoral programs, it would change ratings. Business leaders could refuse to tolerate sexual harassment at work and model respect for women. The church must regain its voice by condemning sin, forgiving repentant offenders, counseling victims of sexual violence, and promoting sexually healthy marriages.

Physicians

To restate our principles, we seek justice, faithfulness, and love; apply God's law to work; promote worthy causes and goals; look for people to serve and protect; and follow the examples of heroes.

The West admires medical personnel because these workers alleviate pain and heal diseases or assist the body as it repairs itself. Physicians have been self-regulating since Hippocrates

---

2. See Salma Hayek's harrowing account of her relationship with a premiere producer in her article, "Harvey Weinstein Is My Monster Too," *New York Times*, December 12, 2017.

3. Charles Taylor, *A Secular Age* (Cambridge, MA: Belknap, 2007), 594–617.

proposed his oath in 400 B.C. The core ideal, to do no harm, included a vow not to assist in abortion or suicide. The physician also promised to "use treatment to help the sick according to [their] ability and judgment." Whether we call it natural law, conscience, or the law of God written on the heart, the Hippocratic Oath offers justice and respect to all patients. When pagan Greeks, Western Christians, and adherents of other faiths agree on essential principles of medical ethics, it implies that God's wisdom is accessible to everyone.

In the language of this book, medical professionals love their patients by striving to restore their health and by treating them as human beings, not diseases or symptoms. They recommend any helpful remedy: better diet, more exercise, less alcohol, fewer medications. They may even encourage the reconciliation of a broken relationship or a return to community.

Gifted physicians and nurses listen patiently, since the sick do not divulge the whole truth at once. Like Jesus, they touch appropriately. Since they know they can harm their patients, they watch themselves. They give the body every opportunity to heal itself. They also know that the medical system "often teaches patients to stay sick, not to get well" and that hospitals can be dangerous places.[4]

This raises a great issue in medicine. Physicians may vow to do no (deliberate) harm, yet they *do* cause harm accidentally. One major study estimates an annual American toll of 250,000 iatrogenic deaths stemming from medical treatments such as unnecessary surgeries, hospital infections, and reactions to medicine.[5] This is hardly the only problem. For instance, patients deserve dignity, yet contemporary treatments bring many an indignity. Again, physicians should care for the whole person, body and soul, but some physicians believe the soul is a fiction.

4. Clifton Meador, *A Little Book of Doctors' Rules* (Philadelphia: Hanley & Belfus, 1992), 264, 266.

5. Barbara Starfield, "Is US Health Really the Best in the World?," *Journal of the American Medical Association* 284, 4 (July 26, 2000): 483–85.

Physicians also face financial temptation: because tests and treatments bring revenue, there is a lure to test and to treat. Physicians also face the familiar desire to follow the crowd and to be caring *as care is defined at that moment*. The current approach to people who identify as transgender may illustrate this. Tragically, due to developmental irregularities *in utero*, a tiny percentage of babies are born with ambiguous genitalia. A larger number of people experience gender dysphoria, the sense that their biology does not match their gender identity. A man senses that he is a woman, locked into a male body, or vice versa. The feeling is real and the stories are potent.[6] The first response to them must be empathy. Imagine the experience of awakening daily, feeling that one has the wrong body. Physicians commonly treat these symptoms with hormone therapy and sometimes with gender-reassignment surgery. Popular literature asserts, "Hormones work. Surgery works."[7] But no well-designed medical study has found that sex reassignment surgery brings *lasting* benefits. Critical meta-reviews have found that studies reporting good results after sex-reassignment surgery suffer serious flaws, including a tendency to lose track of study participants, due in part to "completed suicides" and a short time frame. Meanwhile, "the most comprehensive study," a Swedish project that tracked participants for thirty years, found that suicide rates leapt to 19.1 times the national average after sex-reassignment surgery and that psychiatric hospitalizations nearly triple "even after adjustment for prior psychiatric disease."[8]

In fact, sex- or gender-assignment surgery may be a misnomer,

---

6. See Mark Yarhouse, *Understanding Gender Dysphoria* (Downers Grove, IL: Inter-Varsity, 2015), 86–100. Yarhouse carefully assesses data on the frequency of dysphoria (91–99).

7. Jesse Singal, "Your Child Says She's Trans. She Wants Hormones and Surgery. She's 13," *The Atlantic*, July/August, 2018, 94.

8. "Proposed Decision Memo for Gender Dysphoria and Gender Reassignment Surgery (CAG-00446N)," June 2, 2016, Centers for Medicare and Medicaid Services, https://www.cms.gov/medicare-coverage-database/details/nca-proposed-decision-memo.aspx?NCAId=282.

since sexual differences "manifest themselves in many bodily systems and organs, all the way down to the molecular level." Biological sex shapes people organically "at every level of our being." Surgery and hormones cannot change anyone into the opposite sex. "They can affect appearances . . . [and] outward expressions of our reproductive organization. But they . . . can't turn us from one sex into the other."[9] Needless to say, these assertions are quite unpopular at the moment. But if they are correct, the medical profession needs physicians who will stop providing hormones for people seeking attention and stop performing elective surgeries that have a dubious record. It is daunting to resist a movement that sweeps through a culture, but resistance is true professionalism if the movement brings more harm than good.

The challenges facing physicians are hardly unique. Indeed, the nobler the profession, the greater the temptations and the greater the harm when they go astray. This holds widely. Pastors lose faith, lawyers try to thwart justice, generals attack neighboring nations instead of defending their own, counselors get depressed, and physicians abuse and neglect their bodies. Like everyone, they need godly mentors.

Because the healing arts are so powerful, they must be handled with care, yet the economic aspect of medicine often militates against that. For example, physicians want to listen to patients, but regulations currently give doctors twelve to fifteen minutes per patient, and that virtually prohibits careful listening. *A Little Book of Doctor's Rules* by Clifton Meador, M.D., collects aphorisms on medical care, such as, "Drugs should make patients feel better, not worse" and "You do not have to like a patient, but it sure helps." His notes on diagnosis include this gem:

9. Ryan T. Anderson, "Sex Change: Physically Impossible, Psychosocially Unhelpful, and Philosophically Misguided," *Public Discourse: The Journal of The Witherspoon Institute* (March 5, 2018), https://www.thepublicdiscourse.com/2018/03/21151/; Ryan T. Anderson, *When Harry Became Sally: Responding to the Transgender Moment* (New York: Encounter Books), 2018.

There are three kinds of patients. 1. Those who believe every word you say and do everything you suggest—Be careful what you say and suggest. 2. Those who reflect on what you say, wonder why you said it, ask you questions, and then make up their own minds about what they do—Answer all their questions. 3. Those who disagree with everything you say . . . and state that nothing will help them—Preface every suggestion you make by saying you do not think the treatment will work. Lead them to argue that the treatment will work and it will.[10]

This is remarkably perceptive, and yet the forces that manage medicine make it hard for physicians to practice this today. Meador wrote in 1992; today, diagnosis occurs more often through tests than through interviews, and physicians rarely have time for the discussions Meador recommends. Technological and economic forces bring similar changes everywhere.

Meador's schema elicits an additional caveat. The careful listening that Meador praises must be yoked to the right ethical systems. An empathetic listener may, without proper grounding, conclude that abortion or euthanasia is the best solution to a medical problem. Human insight needs the corrective of divine revelation.

Armed Forces

To review once more, we seek justice, faithfulness, and love; apply God's law widely; promote worthy causes; look for people to serve; and follow the examples of true heroes.

Military forces have the capacity to kill, which seems evil, since all premature death is evil in some sense. But in a world filled with armed and predatory nations, military strength is necessary to deter those who would devour weak states and unprotected lands. A credible defense requires a credible offense.

The principal demand on the military is justice, which has

---

10. Meador, *Little Book of Doctors' Rules*, paragraphs 2, 49, 59, 125.

two elements. The first, called *justice to war*, names the conditions that give nations the moral and legal right to declare war. The second, called *justice in war*, enumerates rules for combat. That is vital since protracted conflict tends to spiral toward "total war," in which any act that degrades the enemy's will or ability to fight will be justified. When that happens, "civilized" nations assault and starve civilians and use weapons that cause massive, indiscriminate death.

Justice to war has five main elements:

1. Combat must have a just cause—a real injury, such as invasion of peaceful lands.
2. A legitimate civil authority must declare war.
3. War must have the right intention—a just peace.
4. War is a last resort, after negotiations and nonlethal pressure fail.
5. War must be proportional to the issues prompting it. The damage of war should not exceed the original injustice. Resistance must not do more harm than good. This includes assessment of the probability of success. If a situation meets all these criteria, it *may* warrant military force.

Even *in war*, love and faithfulness govern the military. Faithful soldiers keep their oaths to protect their people. They love their fellow soldiers, whether superiors, peers, or subordinates. Defensive wars can be loving, because solders love their people by protecting them (Judg. 18:28; 1 Sam. 17). Soldiers can even have inner love for an opposing army. To fire a gun in love, a soldier must see adversaries as human, not subhuman, and take no pleasure in using force against them. Moreover, to resist invaders can be an act of love toward the invaders. When the Nazis invaded Europe, they harmed the Polish, Dutch, and French, but they damaged themselves, too. Germany committed terrible crimes for which they paid bitterly. A generation poured rivers of blood onto its hands. Millions of German soldiers suffered moral corruption and guilt, then death, and the German nation bore economic and territorial losses. How much better *for the Germans*, had the Polish, French, and Dutch defeated them at the start. Successful defensive wars help both the invader and the invaded.

Managers

The single clearest result of my interviews was this: low-level workers—beginners—love managers who respect everyone in the workplace. Good managers are intent on treating low-skill, low-wage workers humanely. They speak gently, they ask questions, they smile, and they draft schedules for gyms and retail stores that are fair and accommodate legitimate needs. They love their staff through small acts of kindness and by forgiving minor mistakes. They don't play favorites or disparage socially awkward workers. One interviewee said, "Every business is a people business. It's imperative to maintain relationships, because nothing good happens without a team."[11]

Educators

Our core principles urge us to be just, faithful, and loving, to apply God's law widely, to promote worthy causes, to serve humanity, and to follow noble examples. Love is central to education, since good teachers love their students as individuals, class size permitting, and love them corporately through well-designed instruction. Superior teachers love to present content and to inculcate skills. Love and justice meet when instructors honestly but gently correct student errors (2 Tim. 2:24–25). They do not threaten or bribe, and they do label successes so students understand what they have done right (Rom. 13:3).[12] Teachers develop minds, so that students know the right answer and *why*

---

11. Yes, this section is brief. Consider it a counter to the voluminous management literature.

12. They echo the work of rulers who "punish those who do evil" and "praise those who do good" (1 Peter 2:14; see also Rom. 13:3).

it is the right answer—so students know the facts and see why they matter. Teachers convey information and skill as authorities require, but they also honor student interests when possible. A good teacher will occasionally say, "Trust me, you need to know this," but he also says, "Tell me what you want to study."

Parents have prime responsibility to train their children. Proverbs 22:6 reads, "Train up a child in the way he should go; even when he is old he will not depart from it." This is not an unconditional promise. Children are still responsible agents. Godly parents and teachers lead children to the right path and make it *easy* to see it. A child's "way" includes discernment of a child's gifts. If a father watches his daughter learn Latin effortlessly, he asks her, "What's next, Mandarin or Arabic?"

My interviewees included a recent college graduate who works for a small communication firm. After eight months on the job, she found herself alone in a room with two women, her CEO and the CEO of a principal client. She reported that she was startled but not nervous: "When I was a child, we had famous authors and musicians in our home a few times. My father said famous people usually have a special talent, but they're basically like everyone else. We just enjoyed them. So it was fine to be with the CEOs. Before long I joined their conversation." As Solomon says, it is good to heed a father's instruction (Prov. 2:1).

But individual aspects of education seem easier to address than the systemic side. Since colonial days, the chief responsibility for public education in America has fallen to the local community. Today, about 45 percent of funding is local, 45 percent is from states, and 10 percent is federal. Since funding for public schools largely rests on local property taxes, poorer districts inescapably have weaker schools, while students in wealthy districts enjoy the smaller classes, superior teachers, and additional resources that correlate with superior educational results. The poorer districts struggle in many ways, including high rates of teacher turnover and teaching from substandard textbooks. Mission creep also hampers their work, as they often feel compelled to remedy deficits in nutrition and family support. No one thinks money alone fixes weak schools, but inadequate funding is a factor. So unless they have extraordinary gifts, the poor typically have less access to education. This does not seem to fulfill the idea that to do justice is to give everyone their due—a concept already found in Plato's work and also reflected in Romans 13:7. It doesn't meet John Rawls's test that inequalities are just only if they bring "compensating benefits for everyone," especially the disadvantaged.[13]

It is possible to reduce the disparity between schools with high and low funding. Minneapolis has revenue-sharing policies that reduce the gap between the most and least prosperous schools. It has also reduced the pockets of extreme poverty. This increases the number of viable neighborhoods, which decreases housing costs overall and makes it is easier for the relatively poor to move into the middle class.[14] To make such a change, parents, educators, politicians, and business leaders had to collaborate and the wealthy had to waive certain privileges. They did so, and by supplying good teachers to poor children, the city got closer to the equal opportunity that Americans profess as their ideal.

In market economics, the restructuring of funding can take many forms. Evidence shows that competition spurs efficiency and innovation. Therefore, it makes sense to promote competition in education, even at the elementary and high school levels. Charter schools have generally been successful in the public school arena. Education grants to parents or guardians would multiply options, especially for poor parents who question the public school system. When qualified private schools (whether religious or secular) begin to win students, we might expect public schools to reform themselves, if only to prevent job loss. At best, more equitable funding will create opportunities for upward mobility among the poor, and competition will spur

13. John Rawls, *A Theory of Justice*, rev. ed. (Cambridge, MA: Belknap, 1999), 14–15.
14. Derek Thompson, "The Miracle of Minneapolis," *The Atlantic*, March 2015. https://www.theatlantic.com/magazine/archive/2015/03/the-miracle-of-minneapolis/384975.

educators to teach their students more effectively. Of course, implementation lies in the hands of teachers, politicians, and parents, who know the most about these matters.

Architects and Builders

I close with building, where my ignorance is, if possible, greater than in the other areas. Therefore, this segment relies on interviews with engineers, architects, designers, and contractors. Fortunately, they agreed on the principles guiding their work. In planning stages, the imagination and practical considerations coexist in creative tension. Architects must draft plans that are feasible, for buildings that can actually be erected and then built at affordable prices. Architects long to innovate—to stretch, even to defy, conventions—yet their first concern is safety. Buildings, bridges, and roads must rest on strong foundations. Everyone is responsible to preserve life (the sixth commandment) by constructing roads that minimize accidents and buildings that withstand storms and earthquakes. Designers ensure that no one gets trapped or lost in interior spaces. This demonstrates love of neighbor and protection of people who get confused (Deut. 22:8). Beyond that, good buildings unite workers and create ideal working conditions. At best, the results are both beautiful and functional.[15]

Builders can produce structures that last for centuries. That requires faithful labor by hundreds of people who tolerate neither shortcut nor compromise. Emma (see her story above) said architects face a distinct temptation: the tension "between doing great work for the Lord . . . and the professional fame resulting from that great work." An architect's work, she continued, "is on display." Architects create urban landscapes that shape the lives of those who review their work daily. She asserts, "For the sake of humanity, we must do great work." But the goal of perfection can lead to "egotistical posturing." All architects, Emma

---

15. Roger Scruton, *Beauty* (New York: Oxford University Press, 2009), 69–79.

noted, must "work for the person who called them and not for personal gain." That said, she would also like to know why God gave water, that life-giving molecule, the ability to cause "mold, mildew, and rot." She also wondered if her work might endure in the new creation. But perhaps we can leave our study there, with a woman who wants to serve the Lord and who also has a few questions. We can stand with her, eager to love God and neighbor and to press on by learning and doing more.

SELECT BIBLIOGRAPHY

Aristotle. *Politics*. Translated by Benjamin Jowett. In *The Basic Works of Aristotle*. Edited by Richard McKeon. New York: Random House, 1941.

Bellah, Robert M., Richard Madsen, William M. Sullivan, Ann Swidler, and Steven M. Tipton. *Habits of the Heart: Individualism and Commitment in American Life*. Berkeley: University of California Press, 1985.

DeKoster, Lester. *Work: The Meaning of Your Life*. Grand Rapids: Christian Library Press, 1982.

Frame, John. *The Doctrine of the Christian Life*. Phillipsburg, NJ: P&R Publishing, 2008.

Friedman, Milton. *Capitalism and Freedom*. Chicago: University of Chicago Press, 1962.

Garber, Steve. *Visions of Vocation: Common Grace for the Common Good*. Downers Grove, IL: InterVarsity, 2014.

Guinness, Os. *The Call: Finding and Fulfilling the Central Purpose of Your Life*. Nashville: Word, 1998.

Hardy, Lee. *The Fabric of This World: Inquiries into Calling, Career Choice, and the Design of Human Work*. Grand Rapids: Eerdmans, 1990.

Hardyman, Julian. *Glory Days: Living the Whole of Your Life for Jesus*. Downers Grove, IL: InterVarsity, 2006.

Hatari, Yuval Noah. "The Capitalist Creed." In *Sapiens: A Brief History of Humankind*, 305–33. New York: Harper Perennial, 2015.

Hunter, James Davison. *To Change the World: The Irony, Tragedy, and Possibility of Christianity in the Late Modern World.* New York: Oxford University Press, 2011.

Keller, Tim. *Every Good Endeavor.* New York: Penguin, 2012.

Luther, Martin. "Temporal Authority: To What Extent It Should Be Obeyed." In *Selected Psalms III*, edited by Walther A. Brandt, 75–129. Vol. 45 of *Luther's Works.* Philadelphia: Muhlenberg, 1962.

———. "Whether Soldiers, Too, Can Be Saved." In *Christian in Society III*, edited by Helmut T. Lehmann, 87–137. Vol. 46 of *Luther's Works.* Philadelphia: Fortress, 1967.

Maslow, Abraham. "A Theory of Human Motivation." *Psychological Review* 50, 4 (1943): 370–96.

Miller, David. *God at Work: The History and Promise of the Faith at Work Movement.* New York: Oxford University Press, 2007.

Nelson, Tom. *Work Matters: Connecting Sunday Worship to Monday Work.* Wheaton, IL: Crossway, 2011.

Pieper, Josef. *Leisure: The Basis of Culture.* Translated by Alexander Dru. Indianapolis, IN: Liberty Fund, 1999.

Rawls, John. *A Theory of Justice.* Rev. ed. Cambridge, MA: Belknap, 1999.

Ridderbos, Herman. *The Coming of the Kingdom.* Philadelphia: Presbyterian and Reformed, 1962.

Russell, Bertrand. "In Praise of Idleness." In *In Praise of Idleness and Other Essays.* London: George Allen and Unwin, 1915.

Ryken, Leland. *Redeeming the Time: A Christian Approach to Work and Leisure.* Grand Rapids: Baker, 1995.

Sayers, Dorothy. *Why Work? An Address Delivered at Eastbourne, April 23rd, 1942.* London: Methuen, 1942.

Schutt, Michael. *Redeeming Law: Christian Calling and the Legal Profession.* Downers Grove, IL: InterVarsity, 2007.

Schuurman, Douglas. *Vocation: Discerning Our Callings in Life.* Grand Rapids: Eerdmans, 2004.

Sherman, Amy. *Kingdom Calling: Vocational Stewardship for the Common Good.* Downers Grove, IL: InterVarsity, 2011.

Smith, Adam. "Introduction and Plan of the Work." In *An Inquiry into the Nature and Causes of the Wealth of Nations*. 2 vols. 1776. Reprint, New Rochelle, NY: Arlington House, 1966.

Taylor, Charles. *A Secular Age*. Cambridge, MA: Harvard University Press, 2007.

———. *Sources of the Self: The Making of the Modern Identity*. Cambridge, MA: Harvard University Press, 1989.

Tilgher, Adriano. *Work: What It Has Meant to Men through the Ages*. New York: Arno Press, 1977.

Veith, Gene Edward, Jr. *God at Work: Your Christian Vocation in All of Life*. Wheaton, IL: Crossway, 2002.

Volf, Miroslav. *Work in the Spirit: Toward a Theology of Work*. Eugene, OR: Wipf and Stock, 1991.

Wingren, Gustaf. *The Christian's Calling: Luther on Vocation*. Translated by Carl Rasmussen. Edinburgh: Oliver & Bond, 1958.

Wolters, Albert M. *Creation Regained: Biblical Basics for a Reformational Worldview*. 2nd ed. Grand Rapids: Eerdmans, 2009.

Wolterstorff, Nicholas. *Until Justice and Peace Embrace*. Grand Rapids: Eerdmans, 1983.

Wright, Christopher J. H. *Old Testament Ethics for the People of God*. Downers Grove, IL: InterVarsity, 2004.

INDEX OF SCRIPTURE

INDEX OF SUBJECTS AND NAMES

Was this book helpful to you?
Consider writing a review online.
The author appreciates your feedback!

Or write to P&R at editorial@prpbooks.com
with your comments. We'd love to hear from you.